Sun Tzu Meets Jesse Livermore
And They Both Win

Arthur Fixed

Sun Tzu Meets Jesse Livermore: And They Both Win
Copyright © 2016 by Arthur Fixed
Published by ST Credit Corporation OÜ, Pärnu Mnt. 10, Tallinn,
Estonia

ISBN-13: 978-1530231805
ISBN-10: 1530231809

TABLE OF CONTENTS

INTRODUCTION

It is up to you. You have a choice. You can take the blue pill and go back to sleep, accept whatever the talking heads on major media tell you, never inquire about the puppet masters or their agenda, and accept the democratic myth. Or, you can take the red pill.

Taking the red pill requires that you read on. Nothing is promised you except the truth, as one anonymous anarchic-capitalist cell explains it. We do not promise happiness or success in personal, political, or financial affairs. You may become less happy. You may regret your decision. Not everyone can handle the truth. Not everyone wants freedom.

How you live is up to you. Slavery is dependent on the consent of the slave. Oppression, to succeed, requires the sanction of the oppressed. No regime, whether democratic, monarchic, socialist, communist, or fascist, can exist for long without the public's consent, irrespective of how that consent is manufactured. If consent is withdrawn, the regime falls.

All empires start to fail when they stop expanding. Empires are profitable while expanding. The loot, new tax slaves, and real estate provide a net profit. Administrative costs overwhelm when expansion stops. The feudal system broke down when it couldn't compete with the productivity of free labor.

It is our intent that reading this book will hasten the day you, your family, your friends, your community, your country, and the world withdraws consent from those who would manipulate you to increase their power. Our intent is subversive. You've been forewarned.

We also intend to offer our readers the opportunity to profit. The truth is certainly a good foundation for any economic activity. Anyone can profit from the truth.

Will Rogers, the famous American humorist of the 1920's and 1930's, once told a reporter that making money in the stock market was

5

easy All you have to do is buy a stock, wait for it to go up, and then sell it for a profit. The journalist asked, "What if the stock doesn't go up?" Will Rogers replied "That's also easy: if the stock doesn't go up, don't buy it."

Can we know what will happen in the future? Is there a reliable system for making predictions, precisely as to time, without them being discounted by the investing public? Is there a system that can reliably predict the financial future and give an investor a significant advantage over others? What would that system look like? What would be its essential components?

What everyone knows is not worth knowing in market timing because the market discounts all known factors into today's price. The key is to know what others do not. Insider trading is one example.

The people controlling corporations have insider information and can therefore trade their company's stock at an advantage to the general public. In most jurisdictions this is a violation of criminal law. However, the prohibition against insider trading does not apply to certain groups; for instance, members of the USA Senate and House of Representatives. They are exempt from this prohibition. They have information concerning what laws will be adopted and therefore who will benefit and who will be harmed by their passing laws and regulations affecting business enterprises. According to publicly disclosed reports, the portfolio investments of US Senators and Representatives perform spectacularly compared to investment norms. On average, when the market is down 10 percent for the year, their portfolios are up 10 percent. It certainly pays to be the law maker. How much of the gain is based on superior information vs. indirect payoff is impossible to decipher. There are many other examples.

To garner extraordinary profit you must first wake up to the truth and understand both the art of war and the laws of economics. We will concern ourselves with opportunities for speculative profits based on government intervention into the free market. This is a study of human action by government personnel as it effects human action in the free market. But first, the art of war and the laws of economics.

CHAPTER I

The Art of War
A Summary and Update

The Art of War is a classic text about military strategy. It is commonly attributed to Sun Tzu, who is thought to have lived in China about 2,500 years ago. Some authorities believe it is a collective work. If so, we hope to add to the collective understanding. It was required reading in all USSR military academies. It is required reading today for anyone who wants to fully understand how governments manufacture consent from those they govern.

Moa Zedong famously observed that all political power comes out of the barrel of a gun. All nation states that have issued sovereign debt claim a monopoly right to initiate the use of coercive force within a geographic area. The military can apply the most force. It is the bedrock of state power, the foundation stone of political power. This is where the promise to pay interest and repay principal on sovereign debt comes from.

Sun Tzu was advisor to the king of a small rural kingdom next to a larger, more developed, and better armed neighbor. The larger kingdom's ruler threatened war unless the smaller submitted to his rule. Having no professional army and only farmers to draft as soldiers, Sun Tzu's king saw no way to resist. Sun Tzu boldly declared that he could make the peasant farmers into soldiers and defeat the army of the much larger kingdom. He claimed he could make soldiers of any group submitted to his authority for training. The king asked, "Anyone?" and Sun Tzu responded, "Yes, anyone." The king argued that his concubines, the most pampered of his household, couldn't be organized into a military group that would obey orders.

Sun Tzu asserted that he could do it and in a short period of time if the concubines were completely under his command. The king submitted his 180 concubines to Sun Tzu's military authority. The concubines were organized into two companies with the first ranking in charge of one and second ranking in charge of the other. Sun Tzu then explained that he was their military commander and would give orders to the two company commanders to march and stop marching based on one drum beat to start and two drum beats to stop. The drum was struck once. The concubines did not march. They looked at each other and giggled. Sun Tzu then said, "If the order is unclear, the officer is at fault. If the order is clear but the soldier does not obey, the soldier is at fault." The drum was again struck once. The concubines did not march. They were only bemused and laughed. Sun Tzu repeated, "If the order is unclear, the officer is at fault. If the order is clear but the soldier does not obey, the soldier is at fault." He then took his sword and killed the company commanders and appointed two new ones in their place. Within a very short time the remaining concubines learned to obey orders and march in military formation. Sun Tzu demonstrated the first rule in military discipline and control:

Military Discipline and the Power of the State is Dependent upon the Willingness to Kill Those Who Won't Submit.

Sun Tzu further taught that the highest art in war is managing to make the enemy submit without having to start the first battle. The most important element for accomplishing this is good intelligence gathering. Good spies are essential. Good double agents are the most valuable asset of all. Their value may be greater than half the army. The enemy will act on what it believes the facts to be. A good double agent can give the desired misinformation that results in victory without a battle or complete defeat of the enemy in battle.

The First Priority of the Military State is to Control Information. The Use of Spies and Double Agents is Essential. Deceit is Central to the Success of the Military State.

Sun Tzu counseled that when the enemy is surrounded, it is proper to engage in protracted negotiation to give the impression that you're willing to stop the battle. If the enemy knows they are surrounded and your intent is to kill them all, they will put up a more forceful battle. If they are deceived into thinking they have a way out, they will not fight as if their lives depended upon it.

Use Psychological Warfare and Terrorist Tactics.

It should always be remembered that the central goal is to affect human action. If the enemy can be demoralized and so lose the will to fight, the battle and war may be won on that alone. Sun Tzu uses the example of an enemy outpost on the perimeter of an area controlled by the army. Each night, the soldiers manning the outpost are sent threatening and misleading messages. They are unable to sleep and at week's end, abandon the outpost.

Always Play to Your Advantage and Make the Enemy Respond to Its Disadvantage.

Guerrilla tactics can be very cost effective. A small mobile force that strikes at the perimeters and withdraws when faced with a conventional battle situation can tie down a much larger force. Bankrupting the enemy may mean there is no army to oppose you in battle.

If You Control the Time and Place of the Battle, You Have Won Before the Battle Starts.

In hand-to-hand battle, it takes half a second to respond but only one tenth of a second to act. If you have the initiative, you have a 400 percent time advantage. If you have set the time and place of the battle, your enemy will have to respond to all the surprises you've organized. This is to your advantage and to his disadvantage. Central to accomplishing this is control over information: good intelligence, spies, double agents, and deception and lastly, coming full circle to the starting point, a willingness to kill those who won't submit.

No serious person disputes that the foregoing is central to the art of war. Some argue it is central to the state. Some have suggested that war power is used primarily against people within the territorial region of a state. The fact that during the 20th century, individual world governments killed more of their own citizens than they killed others' in war certainly supports this position. It is the authors' view that understanding economics will clarify this issue further.

CHAPTER II

Economic Law: The Rule of Law and Freedom

The following is an introduction to the fundamental laws of economics formatted as a hypothetical conversation between military strategist and philosopher, Sun Tzu, and famous stock trader, Jesse Livermore. These concepts are not taught in most schools nor are they acknowledged by major media when reporting or discussing economic policy. It is through their understanding and application that opportunities for outstanding profits are possible.

Sun Tzu: What is economics?

Jesse Livermore: Economics is human action in the field of buying and selling services and products.

ST: What is law?

JL: Law is a rule, a useful description that has some predictive value.

ST: What is economic law?

JL: Economic law concerns human action as it relates to the buying and selling of services and products.

ST: Is economic law a science?

JL: Yes, but since it concerns human action, it is not a physical science.

ST: How do economic laws differ from the laws of physical science?

JL: In the sense that both may be defined as useful descriptions they are exactly the same.

ST: What do you mean by a useful description?

JL: Useful in the sense that they have some predictive value.

ST: Do economic laws have less predictive value than the laws of physical science?

JL: Economic laws have just as much predictive value as the laws of any other science.

ST: Why then isn't economics generally taught as a science?

JL: There are two reasons. 1. It is not possible to measure much having to do with human action as precisely as it is possible to measure matters having to do with physical objects. 2. Economic discourse has been perverted for political purposes.

ST: In what way has economics been perverted by politics?

JL: In much the same way that religion was used during the Middle Ages to sanctify central authority, economics has been used to justify state intervention in the free market. The theory of the divine right of kings has been replaced by the state's promotions of general welfare.

ST: Why isn't it possible to measure human action as precisely as it is possible to measure matters having to do with physical objects?

JL: To the extent that a person does something, it is possible to measure that action. We can, for instance, measure whether a person buys or does not buy something at a particular price and at a particular time.

ST: So what is the problem?

JL: To the extent that economic laws are based on what one person does at a particular time at a particular place there is no problem.

The problem arises when that action is used to predict a different person's action or the same person's action at a different place or time.

ST: Why is this a problem of measurement?

JL: The problem has to do with measuring value. We may know that John paid three dollars for a glass of Coke in New York City on January 1, 2016 but that only means that John valued the Coke at that place and at that time more than he valued the three dollars.

ST: Are all economic valuations then subjective?

JL: Yes. We can report the fact of a price paid or of prices paid as for instance in reporting a market value. We cannot measure the value any one person, much less a group of people, places on, for instance, a glass of Coke except to say, in this instance, John, in New York City, on January 1, 2016, valued it more than three dollars. We can only know ordinal values: the Coke first and the three dollars second.

ST: Doesn't this mean that the study of economic laws has little value?

JL: No. Every science has its limitations. For instance, it would be ill-advised to use the laws of gravity to explain electricity or the economic effects of state monopolies.

ST: What is required in order to postulate or discover economic laws or useful descriptions that have predictive value in the exchange of services and products?

JL: An understanding that all individual action is the product of a choice between subjective valuations of competing alternatives. There is, however, a very important limitation. Since it is impossible to measure the amount of a subjective value or the distance between subjective values, it is impossible to accurately add, subtract, multiply, or divide numerical values as they relate to economic activity.

ST: Why do economists use all sorts of statistical data to measure and predict the money supply, business cycles, interest rates, GDP, etc.?

JL: Most economists are in the service of special interests to justify some intervention into the free market for the benefit of a special interest group or central authority. They need the illusion of certainty. Statistics are used to both obfuscate and justify. They are useful tools of political manipulation. They are not very useful in explaining or predicting because all value is the product of an individual subjective judgment that by its nature cannot be measured except with ordinal numbers.

ST: If it is true that economics is used for political purposes to manipulate, then perhaps I should not waste my time studying economics.

JL: Any science can be misused. Economics is not the only science that's been used for political purposes. Meteorology is another example. But the fact that some people have a political agenda with regard to global warming does not mean we should all abandon the study of weather.

ST: How can I know the truth? How can I know that I am being misinformed about economic matters?

JL: A thing cannot at the same time be and not be. If all value is subjective, then it isn't true that value is dependent upon labor, capital invested, or material input. If it's true that subjective values cannot be accurately measured except by ordinal numbers, then all projections based on adding, subtracting, multiplying, or dividing are inherently unreliable and most likely lies. If, however, the prediction is based on individual subjective value judgments of current or future market participants, then there is a basis for considering the analysis to have

16

some value. This does not mean that a prediction will come true, only that it has a sound grounding.

ST: I want to learn economics. I want to learn useful descriptions that have predictive value concerning the exchange of goods and services. I want to learn how to apply economic laws to predict human behavior for my personal economic well-being. I want to become wealthy. What should I do?

JL: To start, let us confine the discussion to economic laws. Becoming wealthy requires application and that involves a much broader scope of inquiry including personality traits and ethics.

ST: Will you also discuss the broader question concerning how I could use an understanding of economic laws to become wealthy?

JL: Yes, but only if you pass the ethics tests.

ST: Ethics tests? I do not understand.

JL: You will, later.

ST: Okay, I will wait. Let's start with economic laws. Where is the beginning?

JL: For man, in the buying and selling of goods and services, the beginning is a subjective valuation concerning various alternatives. We know this to be true from both observations and introspection. If you wish to dispute this first premise, please say so.

ST: What do we call these subjective valuations of alternatives?

JL: Let's call it a value scale. The first premise is that all value is subjective. The second premise is that people prioritize their values. So, for instance, between three alternatives, there would be a first, second, and third ordinal valuation. We know this to be true from both observation and introspection.

ST: But people make mistakes all of the time. They do things that are bad for them. How can you be sure they have correctly prioritized their values?

JL: By the objective criteria of what is done. If a person only has 150 cents and is offered a Coke, orange juice, or coffee each for 150 cents and he buys the Coke then that proves that, between these three alternatives, he valued the Coke as number one. It is irrelevant that one minute later he regrets his choice and wishes he had bought the coffee. Subjective valuations may change by the second and do not require any logical foundation or agreement with anyone. The only way we can know what they are is through recording individual conduct and that is an objectively measurable criteria.

ST: What is the third economic law?

JL: That the only way we have of measuring anything on an individual's value scale is by recording what a person buys or sells at a particular time and place and therefore the value scale information will be incomplete to the extent that any item on the scale is not bought or sold everywhere and at all times.

ST: Can you summarize the first three laws?

JL: Yes.

1. All value is subjective.

2. People prioritize their values.

3. The measurement of any person's value scale is limited by the amount of objective information we have concerning a person's buy or sell activity.

ST: How is this a science?

JL: Economics can be a science if we apply the scientific method to its study. The conclusions we derive from our study of economics will be valid and true if we start with premises that are true and then correctly apply the laws of logic.

ST: Can controlled experiments be used in economics?

JL: Controlled experiments are problematic due to the issue of measuring value. If the science of economics is based on measurements of overt human actions and limited to expression in ordinal numbers, then the science of economics will be no less scientific than any physical science.

ST: Why is it that economists make so many errors in predicting the future?

JL: All science has its limits. Extending economic laws beyond the boundaries of their own limits is a major error. Remember: All value is subjective, impossible to measure exactly, different for different people, and subject to change over time.

ST: In the 1975 introduction to his book, which at that time was the most widely used college economics textbook, Professor Paul A. Samuelson wrote that the USSR's superior central planning system would result in the USSR's GDP overtaking the USA's GDP before the end of the 20th century. Mr. Samuelson had received the Nobel Prize for economics. Why was this Nobel laureate so wrong?

JL: First, I would like to correct a common error. There is no Nobel Prize for economics. Mr. Nobel did not provide for such a prize in his testament. The economic prize is awarded by a committee of the Swedish parliament associated with administering the testament and is funded by Sweden's taxpayers' money, not Mr. Nobel's testament. It is called the Sveriges Riksbank Prize in Economic Sciences in Memory of Alfred Nobel. It is politically funded and controlled. The politicians have sought to control public perceptions concerning economic policy by attaching themselves to the prestige of Mr. Nobel's testament. They have misused this prestige to promote their own interventionist socialist economic policies. Mr. Samuelson was awarded the prestige of the "Nobel" prize because he served the political interests of the people who controlled the awarding of that prize. Mr. Samuelson called himself a "'modern' economist . . . in the right wing of the Democratic New Deal economists." See: nobelprize.org/nobel_prizes/economics/laureates/1970/samuelson-bio.html.

ST: So, you are telling me that I cannot rely on a recognized authority's predictions?

JL: Yes. And, moreover, I am telling you that the institutions that sanctify what is authority in matters of economics have been corrupted by the political process.

ST: Can you prove this to me using the three fundamental economic laws?

JL: I will try.

ST: Please proceed.

JL: Okay. Let us start with the first principle of logic or mathematics: A thing cannot at the same time be and not be. Either a centrally planned socialist economy, the USSR, is superior, in that it

21

results in a larger GDP than a free market system, the USA, produced over a period of time from 1975 to 2000 or it is not superior in that it does not result in a larger GDP.

ST: Are there two sides to this argument?

JL: Yes. Mr. Samuelson maintained that the central planning socialist model was superior to the disorganized free market. Professors Ludwig von Mises and Murray Rothbard maintained that the central planning socialist model was doomed to failure. See: www.mises.org. Socialist planners could not rationally compute because:

1. All value is subjective.

2. People prioritize their values.

3. The measurement of any person's value scale is limited by the amount of objective information we have concerning a person's buy or sell activity.

ST: That much you set down as the three fundamental economic laws. Are you now going to postulate a fourth economic law or clarify or apply one of the three already discussed?

JL: I will now try to extend the third economic law, clarify it, and apply it.

ST: Remind me again. What was the third economic law?

JL: The measurement of any person's value scale is limited by the amount of objective information we have concerning a person's buy or sell activity.

ST: Are there any additional facts you need to establish in order to proceed?

JL: Yes. Free market pricing signals provide reliable indications of value that business people could rely upon to make decisions concerning what, when, where, and in what quantity to produce goods and services.

Mr. Mises and Mr. Rothbard maintained that the "disorganized" free market pricing mechanism was the essential organizing factor around which rational decision making could be organized because it is the only way values can be measured in useable units of information. Without this free market pricing information the socialist central planner could not make any rational decision concerning what, when, where, and in what quantity to produce goods and services.

ST: So, what does that prove?

JL: The events from 1975 to 2000 seem to prove that Mr. Samuelson was in error and Mr. Mises and Mr. Rothbard were correct.

ST: What do you mean?

JL: It is an undisputed fact that the USSR did not economically overtake the USA. This was in part because socialist central planners were unable to make rational economic decisions. They lacked reliable information concerning values. That much should not be open to serious dispute. The record of USSR error in economic calculations is available to anyone who cares to look at the results in plain view.

ST: I agree that no one can seriously argue to the contrary. But, what does this mean for the science of economics?

JL: The history of the USSR's economic collapse, the results of central planning in Cuba and North Korea, and all of recorded economic history support the premise that the only practical way to get useful information concerning the value of goods and services is by recording the price at which they are bought and sold in a free market. So, to apply rule number three: The ability to measure any person's value scale is limited by the amount of objective information we have concerning a person's buy or sell activity, we may add that if we want the information to be timely and accurate (useful), it must be freely available and not the product of coercion (it must be the product of a free market). If it is coerced, it is likely to be inaccurate and untimely. Only in a free market will the information be readily available as price signals freely made by consenting participants.

ST: Okay, let me see if I understand this correctly. In the case of a national economy, only through the free choice of millions of economic players can the price information provided by their buying and selling activity give useful practical information concerning value. Without this accurate value information it is impossible to make any rational decision concerning what, when, where, and how much to produce. It would seem axiomatic to me that without knowing how much it will cost to produce something and how much it is worth when produced, you could not know if you have added or subtracted value by the proposed economic activity. It would also seem axiomatic that adding value is rational and subtracting value is irrational. That is, if the goal is to increase economic well-being, it is necessary to know the value of what will result from the adoption of any project and this cannot be rationally predicted if you do not have accurate information concerning the value of goods and services . . . How could any rational human being argue to the contrary?

JL: Mr. Samuelson did argue to the contrary.

ST: How do you explain Mr. Samuelson's error?

JL: Let me try by further elaborating on the corrupting influence politics can have on economic discussion.

ST: Please continue.

JL: The institutions that sanctify what is authority in matters of economics have been corrupted by politics.

ST: How have you proved that?

JL: There are two possible and mutually exclusive explanations for Mr. Samuelson's error:

1. He was not intelligent enough to discern the truth or,

2. He was intelligent enough to discern the truth but chose to write a falsehood.

ST: Where are you going with this?

JL: You have stated, "It would seem axiomatic to me that without knowing how much it will cost to produce something or how much it is worth when produced, you could not know if you have added or subtracted value by the proposed economic activity. It would also seem axiomatic that adding value is rational and subtracting value is irrational. That is, if the goal is to increase economic well-being, it is necessary to know the value of what will result from the adoption of any project and this cannot be rationally predicted if you do not have accurate information concerning the value of goods and services . . . How could any rational human being argue to the contrary?"

ST: I think I know where you're headed. Are you saying I conceded the point?

JL: It seems to me that for the purposes of this conversation you have conceded the proposition that a person of normal intelligence would understand that a free market is essential to knowing what the value of goods and services are and therefore essential to rational economic planning. Without rational economic planning the USSR could not overtake the USA economically. Therefore, it follows that there are two possibilities: Mr. Samuelson was not intelligent enough to discern the truth or he was in the service of some political group as a propagandist.

ST: Was there anyone who ever thought Mr. Samuelson was not smart?

JL: I exclude the possibility that Mr. Samuelson was unintelligent. Socialism was doomed to failure from its inception. It contained the seeds of its own destruction. Mr. Samuelson was an intelligent person. From the foregoing, I suggest I have made the case that Mr. Samuelson was awarded the "Nobel" prize for economics by bureaucrats in Sweden, not because he spoke the truth but because he spoke falsehood in the service of socialist bureaucrats and their handlers. This is not to suggest there was any overt knowing conspiracy to lie. Rather, the bureaucrats, politicians, and handlers that control the award process look in the mirror and like what they see and are incapable of sanctifying anyone that does not uphold their socialist views. Mr. Samuelson was politically controlled or motivated to spread erroneous propaganda in the service of a force other than truth. Mr. Samuelson publicly identified himself as a Democratic New Deal economist. Can you imagine a mathematician or biologist identifying himself as a Democratic New Deal mathematician or biologist?

ST: Who else should I not trust to tell me the truth about economics?

JL: Anyone under the influence of government bureaucrats, politicians, or their handlers, anyone who has a self-interest in telling a falsehood, and anyone corrupted by taking money or honor from any of the foregoing. Anyone getting a pay check directly or indirectly from the government is suspect. This includes most professors teaching at government-funded universities. Most private universities also accept government funding for various programs and are therefore suspect. Additionally, many private foundations have come under the influence of collectivist, central planning, one-world government Fabian Socialists.

ST: You paint a very dark picture. Are things really that bad?
JL: No, they are much worse.

ST: Why is that?

JL: It is a matter of incentives. Behind every request to intervene in the free market is a small group that may have much to gain and therefore is willing to spend a lot of time and energy to obtain, for instance, a subsidy to grow sugar beets. On the other hand, there's everyone else who stands to lose a small amount and so is not willing to spend a lot of time, energy, or money to fight the sugar beet growers' request. The sugar beet grower may stand to gain 10,000 euros while each member of the general public may only lose 10 cents per day.

ST: There are people who understand this is wrong. Why don't they do more to prevent it?

JL: Most of the people who understand economics are busy making money in the private sector. Those who do not or cannot often find government or academic jobs. It is unreasonable to expect that people dependent on the good will of government will publish articles calling for a decrease in government funding and authority. Additionally, the private sector businessman is not specifically benefited by a free market. He profits from the difference between the cost to produce and the price at which he can sell. As long as the rules do not change during the process, the businessman has just as much opportunity to profit by the difference between the bid and the ask in a partly socialist system as in a free market system. Indeed, he may have better opportunities for profit if he has political influence in a socialist or partly socialist economic system.

ST: So who is benefited by a free market system?

JL: Everyone in general but no one in particular. Economic laws apply equally to a free market and a partly free market. It is just that the results are different under different conditions. The laws stay the same.

ST: I thought you were going to propose a fourth law that only a free market can provide practical, accurate, and timely information concerning the value of goods and services.

JL: This begins to sound like a value judgment. I do not wish to engage in polemics. Perhaps we can say that based on the existing evidence, the free market system provides the most useful practical information about the value of goods and services so that market participants can make timely and rational decisions. This is inherent in rule number three: the measurement of any person's value scale is limited by the amount of objective information we have concerning a person's buy or sell activity. If we understand that in order for the information to be reliable, buy and sell activity must be freely made and not coerced, we can conclude that free market price signals provide the only known reliable, practical, and useful information concerning value in a working economy.

ST: I am confused, perhaps you can summarize.

JL: Yes.

1. All value is subjective.

2. People prioritize their values.

3. The measurement of any person's value scale is limited by the amount of objective information we have concerning a person's buy or sell activity.

Most of what is published concerning economics is political propaganda. It is deliberately designed to mislead. This includes the Nobel Prize for economics. How, why, and to whom it is awarded have been compromised and corrupted by politics. This corrupting influence pervades almost all reputable establishment institutions including universities and foundations. It is possible to understand what the truth is and what political propaganda is by applying the three fundamental laws of economics. Based on existing evidence, it appears that a free market pricing system is essential to a rational organization of production because it is the only known practical way to get useful information concerning the value of goods and services to market participants. It may be sufficient to say that this is so because all value is subjective. It follows that anyone who tells you that value is dependent on the investment of labor or capital is in error. Furthermore, anyone who adds, subtracts, multiplies, or divides economic statistics to prove that this or that policy to subsidize or prohibit an economic activity will be beneficial for the economy is seeking to mislead you.

ST: So, who can I rely upon to tell me the truth?

JL: You should rely upon yourself. Do you understand the three fundamental principles of economics? Do you dispute that they are true?

ST: I thought I was going to ask the questions.

JL: Okay. Let's leave it at that. What is your next question?

ST: Can you give me a little more help on the issue of where and from whom I can get truthful information to advance my understanding of economics.

JL: Start by reading yesterday's news.

ST: Why?

JL: You can compare what they said would happen to what in fact happened. Then you can know who told the truth and who did not.

ST: Can you give me an example?

JL: Yes: Mr. Samuelson's projection that the USSR would from 1975 by 2000 overtake the USA economically with Mr. Mises' and Mr. Rothbard's prediction that the Soviet economy would collapse.

ST: You have a good point. Clearly, the establishment "Nobel" laureate got it very badly wrong. Tell me more about the people who got it right. How could they know?

JL: They understood and applied the three fundamental principles of economics: 1. All value is subjective. 2. People prioritize their values. 3. The measurement of any person's value scale is limited by the amount of objective information we have concerning a person's buy or sell activity.

They were both members of the Austrian School of Economics. They were both proponents of free market economics. Neither was able to secure a prestigious academic post while Mr. Samuelson was able to.

ST: Do you really mean to imply that there are respected members of the establishment, including "Nobel" laureates, who are really no more than political propagandists?

JL: At this point, it should be clear to everyone that the USSR's Marxist Leninist economists were really no more than political propagandists whose function was to sanctify the communist party's monopoly of political power. Religion was used during the Middle Ages in much the same way to sanctify central authority. Today, economic propaganda is used to justify state intervention in the free market. The theory of the divine right of kings has been replaced by the state's promotions of general welfare. We have nothing to gain and much to lose by closing our eyes to the truth. If you want to learn economic laws, you must be willing to face the truth. Perhaps you will have to unlearn falsehood before you can learn truth. The process may not be pleasant but it will be rewarding.

ST: Okay. I understand the importance of the three fundamental principles of economics, but why have you spent so much time discussing the problem of political propagandists?

JL: It is just as important to recognize a falsehood as it is to know the truth. This is especially useful if everyone else is acting on false information and you know it is false information. This can lead to very interesting situations you can exploit to protect your financial interests and to profit from business and investment opportunities. Knowing when you are being misinformed may be very important. Since most of what's written concerning economic issues is propaganda, it is especially important to correctly classify this information as false. Any one false premise may cause the conclusion to be erroneous. It therefore bears repeating that most of what's written about economic issues is false.

ST: What is the best political system to promote economic well-being?

JL: One that permits and promotes a free market.

ST: Why is that?

JL: A free market is the only known way to get useful, accurate, and timely information concerning the value of goods and services to market participants so they can make timely and rational decisions concerning what, where, and in what quantity to produce goods and services. In addition, private ownership provides the incentive and discipline required for the system to operate efficiently. Having your property at risk to loss provides the required concern while the opportunity to profit provides the required positive motivation.

ST: What is the worst political system to promote economic well-being?

JL: One that does not permit a free market.

ST: But all systems provide for some form of regulation. There is no such thing as a completely free market. Aren't you talking about an abstract utopia?

JL: Freedom is a relative concept. As long as man perceives reality through the five senses, he will experience a duality and an apparent conflict. We understand cold only in relationship to hot, wealth in relationship to poverty, and freedom in relationship to slavery. This does not mean, however, that freedom is a meaningless concept any more than slavery is a meaningless concept. There are measurably significant variations in results dependent on the degree of freedom or lack thereof in any economic system.

ST: So, may we view freedom and slavery as opposite poles on a continuum?

JL: Yes. More freedom is better than less freedom. Slavery is detrimental to increasing economic well-being. Freedom promotes economic well-being.

ST: Can you be more specific?

JL: Every government action that interferes with a free market decreases economic well-being, and every government action that promotes a free market increases economic well-being.

ST: Should governments then stay out of the way and do nothing?

JL: No, there are legitimate actions governments need to take to promote a free market economy.

ST: Like what?

JL: Protecting personal and property rights, enforcing contracts, and promoting civil order. If your neighborhood is ruled by criminal gangs, this will definitely prevent the smooth operation of a free market. The criminal gangs will engage in coercion so that market participants will be unable to freely buy and sell.

ST: So, some government interference in the free market can be good for economic well-being?

JL: No. When government agents put bandits in jail, they are eliminating a source of coercion and an impediment to free economic choice. The enforcement of the rule of law promotes voluntary social interaction and cooperation. Free markets cannot exist without a very healthy respect for the rule of law. That these are relative concepts does not make them any less true. All interference with a free market decreases economic well-being and all promotion of a free market increases economic well-being. Governments have a legitimate role to play in protecting a free market. Protecting is not necessarily interfering.

ST: How do we know when protecting becomes interfering?

JL: The question must be formulated precisely: Does the proposed action promote or interfere with economic freedom? Also, who benefits and who loses in the short term? and in the long term? Generally, governments interfere in the free market by prohibiting or subsidizing and they do so to benefit a small, powerful, well-connected group to the detriment of everyone else.

ST: Why do people permit this if it is detrimental to everyone?

JL: A free market benefits everyone in general and no one in particular. We discussed this earlier, the problem of incentives. The small, powerful, well-connected group with much to gain from a subsidy is prepared to put a lot more effort into getting the subsidy than everyone else who loses just a little.

ST: Is that the only reason?

JL: No. Ignorance is another major reason. People are often fooled by the arguments put forward by those promoting government interventions in the free economy. They may incorrectly believe that the benefits outweigh the costs. This is generally because people have a tendency to look only at the short term benefit to the group being subsidized and ignore the long term results to the recipients of the subsidy and to other groups or everyone else.

ST: Can you give me an example?

JL: Sugar beet growers in the EU get a short-term benefit in the form of a subsidy for growing sugar beets. In the long term they may benefit more if they were forced to find economic activity that produced products or services that a free market system would voluntarily pay for. The public certainly would. The subsidy sugar beet growers receive is minus handling costs for tax collection and disbursement. The subsidy raises the costs to everyone else by higher prices, higher taxes, or both. Furthermore, it misallocates capital. Absent the subsidy, business people would not invest money in growing sugar beets in the EU. Instead, they would invest their capital in producing products and services for which a demand existed without a subsidy.

ST: This is getting very confusing. Can you please simplify the matter for me?

JL: The EU sugar beet growers, the politicians, their handlers, and their paid propagandists argue that the EU sugar beet industry needs to be protected. They point out the benefits to gainful employment and tax receipts to EU countries from keeping this economic activity within the EU. They appeal to our charitable nature and patriotism: Let us help our less fortunate local growers; let us protect them from unfair competition from cheap labor abroad. What they don't point out is the following. There are no free lunches. Every government program has a cost. The government does not produce anything. It only consumes. It must pay for everything it consumes by taxes, borrowing, or inflating the money supply. Either the government taxes everyone to pay for the subsidy, borrows the money to pay for the subsidy, or gets the money to pay for the subsidy by increasing the money supply. The borrowing merely delays when the tax is paid. Inflating the money supply steals the purchasing power of everyone else holding existing currency units and may therefore be viewed as a deceptive tax. Whatever benefit the sugar beet grower gets is more than offset by the cost in increased tax, delayed tax, or deceptive tax. Additionally, there is the cost of administration. The direct cost of administration includes the cost to collect tax revenue and the cost to administer the subsidy program to disburse the subsidy to beet growers.

There is also the cost to the rest of society. If the price of sugar is raised by, for example, imposing an import tariff on sugar produced outside the EU, everyone, including candy manufacturers, is put at a disadvantage. Their costs go up. They are less able to compete with candy manufacturers outside the EU who have a lower cost for sugar. This distortion of free market pricing sends false signals concerning real demand and real costs to market participants. This results in all sorts of market dislocations. Real market demands may not be met because resources are diverted to sugar beet production only because of the subsidy. In addition, it promotes politics over production. It elevates those who divide the production over the producers.

ST: Well, I accept that a free market pricing mechanism is essential to rational decision making and that a free market in the ownership of the means of production is necessary to both hold accountable and motivate management. That you have shown to be the case from the application of the three basic fundamental rules of economics and what we know from the collapse of the USSR and the rest of economic history to date. I cannot find any flaw in your reasoning nor can I dispute any of your premises. Accordingly, so far, I can say that your science is sound. Nevertheless, I am bothered by what I see as a tendency on your part to moralize. You say that inflating the currency is a deceptive tax. Isn't this just a value judgment on your part that has no basis in science?

JL: No. It is an accurate description. The people who already hold the currencies pay by the loss of purchasing power that is now transferred to the newly created currency. Since the general public pays and the government gets to use the newly created money it is correct to call it a tax. It is deceptive in that no one in government ever explains how this works, puts it to a vote, or asks the holders of existing currency for permission to take some of their purchasing power from them.

ST: It seems to me there is a very serious moral issue here. Deception is wrong. Doesn't inflating the money supply amount to stealing?

JL: I will not argue with your characterization. A free market cannot exist without the rule of law and the rule of law cannot exist without a free market.

ST: This is the first time I have ever heard it put that way. Is this an original thought on your part?

JL: I think I am summarizing what should be obvious to everyone.

ST: Let me see if I've got this right. You cannot have a free market without the rule of law because without the rule of law people may be subject to coercion and contracts might not be enforced. A free market presupposes voluntary consensual relations without the initiation of the use of coercive force. Have I got that right?

JL: Yes.

ST: Okay, second half: Why can't the rule of law exist without a free market?

JL: I will start the discussion with a question: Can you name a country that has the rule of law without a free market economy?

ST: There you go again. I am to ask the questions and you are to give the answers, okay?

JL: Very well, what's your next question?

ST: Is there now or has there ever been a country that has or had a civilized rule of law without a free economy?

JL: Relatively speaking, no, if you mean by a civilized rule of law that voluntary contracts are respected and enforced and people are free to live in peace and are not subject to arbitrary state action. The issue is addressed by the definition of a free market. In a free market economy there is freedom for all participants. In the law of the jungle there may be freedom of action for the strongest and lack of freedom for everyone else.

ST: Suppose three rich businessmen get together and form three separate political parties that control the government. Suppose further that they pass laws benefiting themselves exclusively at the expense of everyone else. These laws are passed by parliament, signed by the president, and enforced by the courts, but are they in accord with the rule of law simply because they were enacted and enforced in accordance with the law of the land?

JL: The rule of law supposes something higher than a formal compliance with the law of the land. In your example the political and legal systems are used to take money from the general population and give it to three people.

ST: But, if the government is democratically elected and follows the law as accepted by the majority, isn't that following the rule of law?

JL: Democracy may be described as two wolves and one sheep voting on what to have for dinner. The same analogy applies to the politics of economic issues. The two-wolf majority can vote for a tax that applies only to sheep and benefits that apply only to wolves. This certainly would be democratic and may well follow the law of the land, but is it the rule of law? At what point is the lamb justified in resorting to violent action to protect person or property?

The answer to your question is that it depends on your definition of the rule of law and whether the legitimacy of the rule of law comes from human beings or some higher source. It may be that society predates government and that a government, to be legitimate, must be limited to protecting the person and property of society's members. It may be that if a government goes beyond that, it becomes illegitimate.

ST: Then, isn't it a moral issue?
JL: Yes, it is a moral issue.

ST: So, why are we discussing it? What relevance does it have to economics?
JL: We spent a lot of time discussing how politics have distorted the discussion of economic issues. If most of what passes for economic

discussion is really political propaganda and you understand this, then you are at a significant advantage to people who accept political propaganda as truth and act on it. Understanding that something is false is important. Understanding why people disseminate falsehoods is even more important. In an environment where say over 97 percent of what is written about economic issues is political propaganda, it may be essential for you to remember clearly why this is so. Otherwise, you may be swept away by the propaganda, forget it is propaganda, and do many foolish things, acting on falsehoods as if they were truth. Accordingly, it is essential to clearly understand the moral issue underlying why people disseminate falsehoods as truth.

ST: Okay, so why do people disseminate falsehoods as truth when discussing economic issues?

JL: The problem is that, on a moral level, many people are prepared to steal when given the opportunity. This is especially so when they do not believe they'll be caught or punished. Studies have shown that 80 percent of the general public will steal if provided the opportunity to do so under circumstances in which they think they are not being watched or otherwise held accountable.

ST: From where do you get the 80 percent figure?

JL: There have been numerous studies. Every company running a store, bar, or restaurant is faced with this issue. Studies reveal that the 80 percent cuts across age, education, gender, and ethnicity.

ST: Can you please apply this to the three business people who control the government and enrich themselves at everyone else's expense.

JL: What is the difference between the three business people and the example of the two wolves and one lamb? Most people would immediately understand there is something morally wrong with two wolves voting to eat one lamb for dinner. Is it any less morally wrong to take the lamb's property in this way? Can a majority of cannibals morally put you in a pot to boil your flesh and then eat it? Can they vote to take all or part of your property without your consent? Can a government morally do that which an individual cannot?

ST: But the example of the three business people is different. They were elected by the voters. They had the consent of the voters.

JL: Now you've hit upon the reason why over 97 percent of what is written about economic issues is falsehood.

ST: How is this a moral issue?

JL: The three business people/politicians could not have been elected if they had honestly explained to the voters, "If elected we will pass laws resulting in our economic advantage and your economic disadvantage." They needed to disseminate falsehoods. They needed to lie about economic issues in order to fool the sheep. For instance, they needed to say, "Subsidizing sugar beet growers is good for our economy." The reality is that it may be to the short-term benefit of the sugar beet growers and to everyone else's disadvantage. For this short-term advantage, the sugar beet growers spent time, energy, and money. Some of the money undoubtedly went into the pockets of the three businessmen/politicians. They did not have the consent of the voters. The voters were lied to and misled. An agreement requires knowing consent by at least two parties. A fraudulently obtained agreement is not consensual. Without consent by one party there is no agreement.

ST: So, how could they have obtained the consent of the voters in a morally correct manner?

JL: By honestly disclosing what they intended to do and what the consequences of that would be.

ST: Can you give me more details of such a disclosure?

JL: Yes. They could have said, "We wish to use the instrumentalities of government to pass and administer laws and regulations that benefit us and those who finance our election. You should understand that if you give us this power, we will benefit ourselves at the expense of everyone else. Furthermore, we will support such further intervention in the free market as we determine necessary to buy enough support to maintain our power."

ST: Could any group get elected on such a platform?

JL: Yes, if enough voters believe they are getting more benefit from government intervention than it is costing them and they have low enough moral standards or other priorities.

ST: I find that hard to believe. Can you give me an example?

JL: I will give you two examples: a cannibal tribe in Africa and the Russian Federation. All empires are cannibalistic in tendency. There are many historical instances and current situations where economic well-being is not the determining factor in how a society orders its economy.

ST: I am unclear on your moral point here. Can you please summarize?

JL: Economic propaganda is used to fraudulently obtain the public's consent to a system that benefits those with political power at the expense of those without. The victims are frequently complicit in the fraud in that they consent in the expectation that they will be able to "steal" more in benefits than they have to pay in taxes and obstructionist regulation. Thus, to the extent that the moral standard of the rulers and the ruled is low, this fact supports a system with more intervention in the free market. All sorts of economic falsehoods are disseminated in order to hide what is really happening: stealing.

ST: So, your conclusion please?

JL: A genuinely free market economy cannot exist without a high moral standard as expressed in the rule of law. Who sets that standard may be beyond the scope of this discussion. For some it is self-evident and for others an unproven prejudice that the rule of law comes from an organizing intelligence or creator that is higher than mere human beings. It appears that people who argue for situational ethics also tend to support interventionist policies.

ST: How does this relate to the three fundamental laws of economics?

JL: If action is coerced or fraudulently obtained it may be false and so cannot be reliably used to make rational decisions. It will therefore result in a lower living standard. This relates to the third law. Additionally, it is a major disincentive to market participants.

ST: Relate this again to the moral issue please.

JL: I have sought to explain why the moral issue is important. A low moral standard explains why there is so much falsehood in the discussion of economic issues. If you do not understand this, you may forget that over 97 percent of what is written concerning economic issues is political propaganda. For the beginning student this is the most difficult thing to understand, but it is also the most important. It requires that you honestly look at yourself in the mirror and evaluate your own moral level. You cannot correctly apply economic law to your advantage if you continue to behave at a low moral level, if you are yourself corrupted, for instance, by using the coercive mechanisms of state political power to line your pockets. And to repeat, if you can distinguish the truth from political propaganda and so remember what is false, you will have an advantage over all those acting on falsehood. In this way you can use the knowledge of economic law to your personal economic advantage. The moral issue is central to your personal economic success. You will have great difficulty seeing clearly if you're living a lie.

ST: You are saying that without a high moral standard, I will be unable to see the truth.

JL: Yes.

ST: Is this an economic law?

JL: No. We have now moved from discussing economic laws to how we can profit from using them. The correct application of economic laws to real investment and business situations presents many additional problems.

ST: Earlier you said you would teach me how to apply economic laws to my personal financial advantage but only if I passed a moral test. Have I passed it?

JL: No. The test is not an abstraction. It must be understood and passed in the real world of human action. It is not what I say but what you do that determines the issue.

ST: I do not believe I need to have a high moral standard to make a lot of money. Take the example of the three businessmen with three political parties who pass laws favorable to their economic interests. They can become very rich without high moral standards. They have very low moral standards yet they can become very rich indeed.

JL: You are right that they can become very rich. You are wrong in characterizing them as businessmen. They are not making money based on economic principles. They are making money based on theft. Our discussion here deals with the issue of how to apply economic laws in order to become wealthy. If you wish to study the laws of how to become wealthy by theft, I suggest you start by reading *The Art of War* by Sun Tzu and *The Prince* by Machiavelli.

ST: Are you suggesting that I don't have a high enough moral standard to apply economic laws to become wealthy?

JL: No. I am pointing out that there are two altogether different roads to wealth and that altogether different rules apply to each.

ST: No one is a saint. Can I travel a middle road?

JL: Perhaps we all do. Perhaps every time we are less than moral, we are less able to see the truth. Perhaps the loss from being unable to see the truth is greater than the gain we have from living with falsehood. Perhaps we only harm ourselves when we engage in force or fraud. Perhaps there is a creator to whom we will have to give an accounting.

ST: Perhaps I need more moral guidance than economic education?

JL: If you want to be successful, you need both. The same applies to the broader question of the economy. You cannot have a free market without the rule of law and you cannot have the rule of law without a free market. The moral issue inherent in the concept of the rule of law is unavoidable. The study of economics concerns what people do in buying and selling goods and services, and moral issues affect people's behavior in that buying and selling of goods and services.

ST: Are you saying that without a high moral standard I cannot successfully use economic law to become wealthy?

JL: No, I am saying that it will be harder.

ST: How does this relate to economic law as you have expressed it in the three basic principles?

1. All value is subjective.

2. People prioritize their values.

3. The measurement of any person's value scale is limited by the amount of objective information we have concerning a person's buy and sell activity.

JL: Each of these principles is true and 97 percent of what passes for economic discussion is false. In coming to any conclusion concerning an economic issue you must form premises in a logical construct to have a valid conclusion. In order for the conclusion, in addition to being valid, to also be true, the premises must be true. Living a lie may result in your mind fooling you into thinking that a lie is true, and that will result in error. A high moral standard for your own conduct will help you see the truth about everyone else's conduct. A low moral standard and the truth do not appear to go together. How difficult will it be for you to see the truth in the application of all three laws to the problem at hand when 97 percent of what you are told is false?

ST: What is the mathematical probability?

JL: .000027 if we have a 3 percent chance cumulatively three times $(.03 \times .03 = .009 \times .03 = .000027)$.

ST: It seems that I have virtually no possibility of coming to the right conclusion about an economic issue unless I have a high moral standard. Is that what you're saying?

JL: The odds are very much against you. Using the math above, your chances are only 7 in 37,037.

ST: For financial and business success, how important is integrity?

JL: I believe that the three most important things for business success are integrity, integrity, and integrity. Being honest will help to keep your own analysis honest. A reputation for integrity will assure you a constant flow of people who want to do business with you.

ST: Are we still discussing economic laws?

JL: What should now be clear from our discussion of the three fundamental laws of economics is that they all concern the subjective states of individual human beings. So does the issue of integrity. Lack of integrity interferes with the smooth working of economic laws because it interferes with the peace and harmony of people's subjective states.

ST: Are you proposing another economic law?

JL: Yes. Let us call this the first law of applied economics.

ST: What is the first law of applied economics?

JL: Personal integrity advances the peace and harmony of people's subjective states and so promotes the correct application of economic laws. Dishonesty destroys harmony and so makes the correct application of economic laws more difficult.

ST: Is this a universal law?

JL: I do not understand your question.

ST: Where or when does it not apply?

JL: The more advanced the division of labor, the more it applies. Perhaps in a primitive tribe, it would be more effective to be a good hunter, one who misleads and then kills the prey. The more advanced an economy is, the more division of labor and the more dependent people are on others honestly fulfilling their promises.

ST: So, integrity is central to effective economic interaction in an advanced economy?

JL: Yes. It is central to the rule of law. The opposite may be required in war.

ST: Can you connect this for me to economic law?

JL: Integrity is essential to the rule of law and the rule of law is essential to a prosperous economy because without the rule of law we would not have practical useful information concerning the price of goods and services and so be unable to plan rationally. So, since integrity is essential to rational planning and rational planning is essential to a prosperous economy, it follows that integrity is essential to a prosperous economy.

ST: Is integrity then essential for the advantageous operation of economic law at the community level and the personal level?

JL: Yes. All of this is inherent in the third law, the measurement of any person's value scale is limited by the amount of objective information we have concerning a person's buy or sell activity.

ST: What causes inflation?

JL: Inflation is caused by increasing the money supply.

ST: I thought that inflation was an increase in prices. Isn't that the case?

JL: The traditional definition of inflation is an increase in the currency units, and that causes an increase in prices.

ST: Can prices go down while there is an increase in the money supply?

JL: Yes, if the increase in currency units is less than the increase in production of goods and services.

ST: When would there be a decrease in prices?

JL: If there was no increase in the money supply and there was a two percent increase in production, there would be roughly a two percent decrease in prices.

ST: Is deflation bad?

JL: That depends on your personal financial position. In the last example where the money supply stayed constant and there was a two percent increase in productivity, everyone would benefit equally from a two percent decrease in prices. Borrowers, however, might find it two percent more difficult to pay off their debt as the real value of money increases by two percent. Then again, in a society that expected a two percent deflation rate, that fact would be factored into the cost of credit and so the interest rate may be lower than when there was a two percent inflation rate.

ST: I'm interested in learning more economic laws that I can apply to advance my economic well-being. I am not really interested in the mechanics of inflation rate computations. Please teach me more applied laws of economics. Perhaps you think I am not ready to learn more applied laws?

JL: A theoretical framework laid out in an orderly manner may provide a useful analytical tool. You should understand what is before you decide what to do about it.

ST: Good point; so what should I understand next?

JL: Concerning inflation you should understand what does not cause it.

ST: Why is that important?

JL: Because 97 percent of what is written about inflation is a deliberate attempt to mislead.

ST: So, what does not cause consumer price inflation?

JL: Everything except an increase in the supply of money. Inflation is not caused by an increase in the price of oil, labor, interest rates, etc. It is not caused by a wage price spiral.

ST: If that is so, why is so much said and written about the wage price spiral, etc.?

JL: In order to deflect attention from the fact that politically powerful forces are stealing.

ST: Stealing what and from whom?

JL: Stealing the purchasing power of existing money held by its existing owners.

ST: Can you clarify please? I do not understand how this happens.

JL: You are not supposed to understand. If everyone did, it would be impossible for the thieves to get away with the theft. Let's say there are 100 people on an island and all are producing and trading their excess production. Let us further assume that they use USA dollars as a medium of exchange and that the total money supply is $100,000 or $1,000 per person. Now suppose one of the 100 people on this island is a printer and he prints an additional $100,000 and uses it to buy goods and services from the other 99 people on the island. Everyone would understand this counterfeiting to be theft. Now suppose we have a 300-million-person economy and the government or a private central bank with government backing increases the money supply by three percent each year and does so by expanding credit through the banking system. Is this theft? Is it theft on a smaller or on a larger scale?

ST: Are you referring to the USA?
JL: Yes.

ST: Are you suggesting that the USA has a private central bank?

JL: It is a fact that the Federal Reserve System is privately owned by the large commercial banks in the USA.

ST: How is the USA dollar inflated by the Federal Reserve?

JL: By the creation of credit through bookkeeping entries. Credit is money. Literally, they create money or credit out of thin air. The system is deliberately difficult to understand so the public won't object to the theft of purchasing power from holders of the existing money supply. Almost everything about the system is a lie starting with the name Federal. This gives the impression that it is a governmental agency. It is not. It is privately owned, controlled, and operated for the benefit of its private owners. It is a private cartel operated for the benefit of the cartel members.

ST: I am shocked. How could such a thing happen?

JL: The central banks of both the UK and France were privately owned until after WWII. The cartel or monopoly power to issue a nation's money has throughout history been the most sought after and fought over of all political privileges. The Federal Reserve is the third time the USA has had a private central bank. The first and second were closed down by presidents Jefferson and Jackson respectively. You should not be shocked. Most of what is written about economics is designed to advance the interests of politically powerful groups. It is not truth. It is designed to mislead. If you are still shocked then you do not yet fully understand our prior Q and A.

ST: How does this fit into the laws of economics?

JL: We've discussed how integrity is essential to the advancement of economic prosperity because of the need for useful information concerning value and the limitation on that information as expressed in the third law of economics. You may recall that what we know about a person's value scale is limited to what we know concerning what has been bought or sold. This is complicated by a manipulative system developed to hide a constant theft of purchasing power from the holders of existing money. Money is one half the value of every transaction. How can the real value of anything be known if the value of money is continually manipulated? In answer to this problem, I propose a law of applied economics as follows. In the application of any law of economics it is essential to determine the truthfulness of each premise used to come to a correct conclusion. Furthermore, since so much of what is written is a deliberate plan to mislead, it is essential to know the motivation of the party providing the information. So, in the practical use of economic laws it is essential to know the motivation of anyone providing information in order to properly determine the reliability of that information.

ST: Do we need to know any facts beyond what people buy and sell?

JL: The price at which people buy or sell is an objective standard only if there is a consistently reliable unit of measure. When money is tied to a commodity there is a basis. When it is tied to debt, it is a promise without a connection to a commodity and so without any basis except the police power of the state enforcing legal tender laws.

ST: Are you saying that unless there is a commodity-backed currency, the information expressed in currency units is unreliable?

JL: Yes.

ST: How does that relate to your second law of applied economics: In the practical use of economic laws it is essential to know the motivation of anyone providing information so that you may properly determine the reliability of that information?

JL: Perhaps it may be helpful to ask the following question. What is the reliability of information expressed in fiat currency and what is the motivation of the people who have imposed a fiat currency regime to supplant a commodity-backed currency? Since half the value of every

51

transaction is expressed in currency terms the issue is very important to the study of economics.

ST: You are not making sense. The average person does not consider the issue at all. He just uses whatever currency is required. Please clarify.

JL: You are correct as far as you go. The average person does not consider the issue, but that is because he's accustomed to having the possible use of force and fraud imposed on him to compel his use of fiat currencies.

ST: What force and fraud?

JL: Fiat currencies continue to be accepted in the market place because at one time they were tied to a gold standard. The modern banking system can be traced to the goldsmiths of Vienna, Italy during the 1500's. Merchants would deposit their gold for safekeeping with goldsmiths and the goldsmiths would give merchants paper receipts for the deposited gold. The merchants started to use the paper receipts for the gold in commercial transactions. This was easier for the merchants than physically delivering gold. Soon the goldsmiths started to issue more receipts than they had gold, and so the fractional reserve banking system got its start. Fraud occurred when the goldsmiths issued more receipts than they had gold on deposit. They could do this because only a small number of their clients asked for the delivery of their gold at any one time. The force occurred when governments passed legal tender laws requiring creditors to accept paper instead of gold in the payment of debt.

ST: I am having great difficulty following your point. Please explain in more easily understandable terms.

JL: I will try with another historical example: the year 1066. That was the year William the Conqueror left Normandy, now northern

France, with an invading force to overtake England. William declared himself king, took control of all the land, and demanded tribute from the Anglo Saxons and Celts. If tribute was not paid to the military representing the Normans, the local population was very badly sanctioned. In time the tribute was called taxes and the military was replaced by bureaucrats called tax collectors. If you read the Magna Carta, which defines the rights of Englishmen, you will find roughly the following. The Lord created the earth. JC is the Lord's only begotten son. The pope is JC's representative on earth. The pope granted England to the king of England in return for payment and loyalty. The King granted parts of England to the noblemen in return for payments and loyalty. Therefore the peasants living on the land of the noblemen must pay taxes because they are ruled by divine right.

In order to make it easier to collect tribute the peasants were taught that this was their religious duty. Collection in monetary units rather than eggs, milk, wheat, etc. further simplified the process and provided an additional opportunity to hide the fact that a new ruling class was taking by force. Direct application of brute force is very costly and inefficient. It is much easier to steal by deception. Also, taking once amounts to much less than what can be collected over a period of years. And so we have in every modern society a group that may be characterized as net tax payers and a second group that may be characterized as net tax receivers. The elite of the net tax receivers are generally referred to as the establishment and they are the ones that control the government. It is generally not possible for them to continue in their privileged position when a majority understands what is really happening. Therefore, all forms of deception are used to hide the truth. That is why 97 percent of what is written about economics is falsehood. This includes what is written about inflation and the monetary system.

ST: Please relate this back again to inflation.

JL: Inflation is an increase in the supply of money. Money includes credit. The new money takes purchasing power away from existing money. The holders of existing money lose. The recipients of new money gain. If there is a private central bank permitted to create new money at will out of thin air, it has the ability to steal all the liquid and most of the non-liquid wealth of the society where the monetary units being inflated is used. In an advanced economy, the people with the power to issue a society's money at will are the true rulers. Everyone else is paying them tribute, and most people do so without knowing it.

ST: So maybe the third law of applied economics should say something about the importance of knowing the truth?

JL: I propose the following laws of applied economics.

The first law of applied economies is: Personal integrity is essential. This is because personal integrity advances the peace and harmony of people's subjective states and so promotes the correct application of economic laws. Dishonesty destroys harmony and so makes the correct application of economic laws more difficult. The second law of applied economics is: Know the motivation of people providing you with information. In the practical use of economic laws it is essential to know the motivation of anyone providing information so that you may properly determine the reliability of that information. Remember that 97 percent of what is written about economic matters is intended to mislead you. The third law of applied economics is: Value, exalt, and verify the truth absolutely. The common thread is to prevent the acceptance of a false premise as this would make the conclusion unreliable.

ST: All three laws of applied economics have to do with the truthfulness of the premises in applying the three fundamental laws of economics. Can't we just say that truthfulness in the application of the fundamental laws of economics is essential when applying the fundamental laws?

JL: Yes. The first law, integrity, has to do with the truthfulness of the person applying the fundamental laws of economics. The second is concerned with the truthfulness of people providing you with information and the third with verifying the truthfulness of the first two. The critical point is that if your premises are correct, that is truthful, and you correctly, that is logically, apply the fundamental laws of economics, then your conclusions will be correct in that they will be both valid and truthful.

CHAPTER III

Private Trusts, Foundations, and Corporations
An Application of the Fundamental Laws of Economics for Financial Benefit

The reader should not take any of this chapter to be a recommendation or even a suggestion. Laws are always changing. If we had a perfect solution, we wouldn't publish it as that would insure a change in the law and regulation to make it illegal or impractical. The methods discussed here have worked in certain jurisdictions in the past. This chapter should be read in the context of some private people's responses to adverse state and private actions. The solutions examined primarily concern privacy and control over investment activity using trusts but apply equally to properly structured corporations, LLCs, partnerships, foundations, and joint venture companies.

Foreign Trusts and Joint Venture Companies

There are many uses for an international trust or company. It can buy, hold, and sell property for the grantor. It can operate a business. What a trust can do is limited only by imagination.

Case history: WILLIAM HUGHES (K.C.B.)

Sir William Hughes is a 68-year-old retired solicitor living in London. He gave up his successful law practice three years ago after suffering a heart attack but has continued to earn income as a part-time investment advisor and from rents on commercial property he owns. He and his wife, Edna, have four grown daughters and six grandchildren. Even though Sir William considers himself to be a loyal Englishman (he received three citations for bravery while serving as an RAF pilot), he does not wish to see his estate eaten up upon his death by England's confiscatory death duties. Since Sir William's wealth is composed largely of income-producing real property, his estate is especially susceptible to assessment. In addition to these foreseeable estate and inheritance taxes, the pressure from income taxes on his securities trading, investment counseling fees, and rental income have become increasingly onerous.

Hughes' Trust

The first problem Sir William addresses with his new trust is the vulnerability of his commercial property to inheritance confiscation. To reduce this risk, he first forms a domestic corporation, Britannia Properties, authorized to issue 10,000,000 shares. Sir William contributes all his commercial rental properties, worth approximately £500,000 to Britannia Properties in exchange for 1,000,000 shares and gives each daughter 200,000 shares. The other 9,000,000 shares are issued to Island Enterprises for a total purchase price of £450,000 plus promissory notes.

Island Enterprises is, of course, none other than Sir William's private family trust. When the Hughes die, their visible estate will contain little more than the 200,000 shares of Britannia Properties which are equal to a fraction of the value of the original rental properties. The Hughes' invisible estate, held in the private trust, will be discreetly made available to Sir William's heirs in accordance with his instructions to his trustee.

To secure a favorable mortgage for purchase of additional rental properties, Sir William employs his trust in another fashion. Britannia Properties borrows £250,000 from the trustee/trust, which is acting as undisclosed agent for Sir William's private trust. The loan funds, which were borrowed for ten years, are then placed with the trustee trust's investment department. The trust is given discretion to invest in securities with these funds. At the time, the trustee trades for an investment account belonging to the trust. The trust's investments generally experience capital gains while the trust supplies Britannia Properties with documentation of tax-deductible capital losses.

As a result of the foregoing set of transactions, Sir William derives a £250,000 balance sheet item, loan-expense deductions, investment-loss credits, and capital losses for his domestic company; and capital gains for his private trust. At the end of the loan term, Britannia Properties may choose to roll over the loan for another ten years under the same terms or it may issue stock in payment, thus moving an even greater percentage of equity offshore. All this was made possible by a net interest fee of two percent paid to the trustee trust, plus brokerage fees.

Finally, Sir William uses his trust to aid him in his personal investment trading. Hughes' trust, using the name Carib Investment Fund, hires him to act as its investment advisor. Sir William is given complete authority to trade on Carib's account. As a result, otherwise taxable profits can be expatriated to the "foreign" investor.

Case history: DEBORAH KATZ

Deborah Katz is a 31-year-old single businesswoman. She lives in Haifa, Israel and owns a small but growing import export business. Before-tax profits have been good, but Israel's defense-dominated economy has exacted its tribute in crushing taxes and inflation. Katz's ability to do foreign business is hampered by the size of her company and Israel's currency controls.

Katz has always had an interest in handcrafted items produced in Arab countries but her gender and nationality keep her from fully capitalizing on that interest in her import export business.

Katz's Trust

Freedom of action and increased profits are Katz's reasons for acquiring a secret offshore trust. Katz gets things rolling by mailing a number of money orders, purchased anonymously at various locations, to her trustee. She then instructs the trustee to form a Cypriot corporation, Mid-East Trading, Inc., to be held by the trust in the form of bearer shares. Katz arranges with the trustee to partially manage the trading company. Management duties include having the trustee's associate office in London hire two business agents, Simon Field and Omar Anwar, to act on behalf of Mid-East Trading in Islamic countries. Neither Field nor Anwar is aware that he is working for an Israeli woman. As far as they know, their employer is a British antique dealer whose interests are represented by a Caribbean investment trust.

The foreign trading company operates independently of Katz's Haifa import export business and has deals all over the world. The only significant contact between the two businesses is when one is selling goods to the other. A substantial percentage of the Haifa company's business is represented by these transactions. They are invariably favorable to Mid-East Trading, Inc., so much so that after expenses, the Haifa company has only negligible profits and little or no income tax liability. On the other hand, the offshore trading company has high, tax-free profits. The profits that aren't plowed back into the business are invested worldwide in hard assets, especially gold. The company has diversified holdings in Zurich, London, New York, and Hong Kong.

Since Katz got her private trust, she has been quite content to keep her domestic profile low while her trust-owned international business flourishes. Her eventual plan is to be hired by Mid-East Trading, Inc. as an international buying agent. As such, Katz plans to combine business with pleasure and fulfill her lifelong ambition to travel and see the world in luxury.

Case history: GILLES AND ANNE DURAND

The Durands consider themselves typical French Canadians. They are proud of their French cultural heritage and take an active role in Montreal community life. Nevertheless, they have mixed feelings about the possibility of Quebec's independence from the rest of Canada. Both Gilles and Anne have to work very hard to make ends meet.

Gilles, 36, fears that his job as an autoworker is especially vulnerable in light of world economic conditions. Anne works as a housecleaner and notices that four of the homes she cleans belong to English-speaking families. To help augment the family income, Gilles works on cars for people who answer his classified ads. Gilles trades his car repair services for tuition at an underground English school where their daughter Claudine studies. Gilles and Anne consider it important that Claudine be comfortable in both languages so that she will be able to find a job in a tight market. Anne and Claudine contribute to the family income by buying underpriced items at garage sales and reselling them at various flea markets in the area. For fun, the family regularly goes on camping trips to Vermont. Two or three times a year, Gilles and Anne go to New York City to shop and see Broadway shows.

The Durands' Trust

Because they aren't wealthy, the Durands feel that it is important for them to take care of what they do have. They want to use the trust as an emergency reserve as well as for their retirement. Additionally, they want to save for Claudine's college education and to provide something for her when they are no longer around. They want to do this without the bite of provincial and federal tax collectors. As working people, they resent the burgeoning trend toward economic redistribution in favor of tax consumers. They resent their tax money being spent on people who do not want to work.

To fund their trust, the Durands periodically take unreported cash from Gilles's private auto repairs, Anne's housecleaning, and flea market sales and wire it to their Caribbean trustee while on Vermont camping trips or New York visits. Using this underground payroll savings plan, they are able to regularly and safely put away savings.

The instructions and discretion given to the trust are broad. The trustee is directed to invest one third of the funds in hard money investments such as gold mining stocks. For patriotic reasons, they have the trustee invest another third in stocks and bonds of Quebec corporations. The remaining third is held in interest-bearing accounts denominated in a market basket of strong currencies. Within these broad criteria, the trustee can exercise discretion as to the particular securities and currencies to be held.

During their lifetime, Gilles and Anne retain full control over the distribution of trust funds. In the event of both their deaths, the trustee is to distribute the assets to Claudine upon her twenty-eighth birthday, earlier if, in the opinion of the trustee, Claudine is in sufficient financial need.

Case history: ALICIA MOORE

Alicia Moore is a 48-year-old businesswoman. She owns a successful advertising agency in Southern California. She has two daughters attending Harvard University who are bound for long and expensive courses of graduate study (Medicine and Astrophysics). She worked for years to put her husband through school but he deserted her twenty years ago, leaving her penniless and unemployed. She only got around to obtaining a divorce a year ago. Since she has been on her own, she has built a profitable business and a net worth of more than US$ 5 million, most of it in real estate.

Moore recently fell in love with a 25-year-old Ph.D. candidate (Mathematics) and would like to marry again, but she has certain worries. She doesn't want to place herself in the position of being dependent on a man ever again. She also wants to finance the best possible education for her daughters to give them an independent start in life. She hopes to leave a substantial estate to them when she dies.

Moore worries that her former husband may learn of her good fortune and try to cash in on it since they were legally married in a community property state while she was accumulating her money. She is aware that the California courts are noted for strange rulings in the area of domestic relations law. Her current romance sparks similar concerns.

Moore believes that everyone concerned is better off if she keeps her true net worth to herself and does not spread temptation. She has always had a natural sense of privacy and keeps her personal affairs to herself, so the extent of her financial success is not generally known. She now seeks a way to further safeguard her assets.

Moore has decided to get out of the real estate investment business because she believes that the greatest growth opportunities for the future lie in other investments. The spread of rent control laws worries her and she fears that tenants' growing militancy will eventually lead to the effective confiscation of her property. The illiquidity of real estate investments bothers her, as well as the fact that direct real property ownership leaves her assets exposed to anyone who attempts to sue her.

Moore's Trust

Alicia Moore sells all of her real estate holdings over the course of a year. She pays capital gains taxes on the sale proceeds and then transfers the funds to her foreign trust. She lays out a diversified investment program for the trustee and directs the trust assets be transferred to the control of her daughters upon her death. Moore does not need the trust assets to live on. She intends to allow them to accumulate for retirement and for her children. She watches investment performance and occasionally suggests changes. She also adds to her trust from time to time from her business income. She is able to relax in her personal and professional life, knowing that she has some assets that are insulated from day-to-day life in a complex and litigious society.

Case history: RONALD SMITH

Unfortunately, not everyone wants a foreign trust for purely defensive reasons. The following case history chronicles the use of a private trust as a vehicle for official misfeasance and abuse of public trust.

Ronald Smith is a career civil servant. Though he started out as an office clerk with the Securities and Exchange Commission (SEC), he quickly rose in status after a politically advantageous marriage into a well-known Texas family. His father-in-law, the head of a television and radio empire and a canny influence peddler, used his political clout to land Smith a high position in the SEC hierarchy. Smith sees the great potential for personal gain inherent in his official powers. Because these opportunities require sensitive negotiations and surreptitious exchanges, Ronald seeks the secrecy of a foreign trust.

Smith's Trust

Smith has two main uses for his private trust, one passive and one active. On the passive side, he instructs the trustee to accept deposits made on his behalf and hold them in Swiss Francs until needed for other purposes. The sources of these deposits are legitimate and not-so-legitimate businessmen who wish to avoid interminable delays and technical challenges to their securities transactions. This is accomplished by first harassing the victim with numerous (but always legally permissible) delays, challenges, and official foot-dragging tactics. When the inevitable inquiry comes as to what can be done to facilitate matters, Smith hints that a sizable consultation fee paid to a certain numbered account in the Caribbean can get things moving. And it always does.

Smith actively uses his trust in another, safer way. He discovers that he can easily obtain confidential and proprietary information from publicly held companies. With enough inside information, he could very profitably buy tradable securities through his offshore trust. Other market forces often move securities counter to the direction predicted by these data, but Smith ingeniously finds an answer to these obstacles: his final solution.

Smith and his SEC cronies had watched with jaundiced eyes as gold and gold securities increased in value. But Smith sees an opportunity for profit. He realizes that he doesn't have to wait for the market to move but can make it move as he wants. For several weeks Smith uses his influence to convince others in his department that a full-scale investigation of securities practices in gold mining shares is long overdue. He instructs the trustee of his trust to take a massive short position in gold mining shares. Thereafter, he heavily mortgages his home, summer home, and yacht, and he moves those funds offshore to further bolster his short position. His colleagues give him carte blanche in spearheading what they dub "Project Fool's Gold." On the Friday preceding the Monday on which Smith plans to announce the investigation, he is feeling good. Every cent he has is poised to take advantage of gold's decline. That day, however, the Government Accounting Office orders an unannounced audit, and Smith is assigned to work on the SEC response. Project Fool's Gold is temporarily shelved and all employees are sequestered to work on the audit. Meanwhile, there is an unexpected rise in the price of gold due to strategic stockpile purchases by the Chinese government. Without warning, Smith's heavily leveraged position is wiped out. Smith is ruined.

CHAPTER IV

The Money Illusion

In the historical context, freedom is a new idea. For the greater part of recorded history, perhaps 97 percent of the time, tyranny has ruled men's lives. Sun Tzu was popular 2,500 years ago and still is today while Ludwig von Mises received only a passing mention in the last century. Though one explored the science of war and the other the science of economics, both writers clearly understood the importance of individual human action. Only individuals act. Individual action may result in certain groupings but the group called government is a fiction. There are bureaucrats, politicians, and their paymasters. They individually act. The government as such is a legal fiction.

How does this group of individuals called government promote and maintain its fictive elevated status? How does it finance itself? In large part, the answer lies in the money illusion.

The money illusion is the belief that government can augment overall economic well-being by increasing a nation's money supply,

Now consider the following analogy. Is it possible to increase the water level of a swimming pool by taking water from one end and pouring it into the other? The answer is evident: Obviously not. Any water taken from the south end draws water from the north, east, and west ends. In fact, this operation will always produce a net loss due to the cost of moving water from one end to the other and the physical loss of water incurred while handling.

Government subsidies are nothing more than another example of resource redistribution. Governments take money earned by the private sector and give it to approved projects, public and private. No new wealth is created, just as the water level does not rise in the swimming pool.

If A, B, and C are taxed to give a subsidy to Z, it is clear that the overall wealth of A, B, C, and Z has not increased. A portion of A, B, and C's wealth has simply been moved to Z. To argue that this is a net benefit to society presupposes that politicians and bureaucrats are more competent decision makers than individuals operating in a free market. It elevates political coercion over individual freedom.

To finance their programs, governments have three sources of income: taxes, borrowing, and inflating the money supply. Taxes are taken under threat of force and borrowing is a delayed tax that must be paid with interest, while inflation increases the money supply thereby lowering the value of existing monetary units. When the state spends borrowed money, it consumes wealth it did not create in just the same way it spends money raised by taxation. Government borrowing is generally facilitated by the third income source, monetary inflation.

This can be accomplished in one of two ways: by printing money or by creating bookkeeping entries when extending credit. In the case of credit, new money is created as follows. A borrower signs a promissory note for x amount. The bank takes the note and, on its books, credits the borrower's account for x amount. This bookkeeping entry is then treated as a money equivalent and is traded back and forth within the banking system so that the original x amount multiplies. The illusive bookkeeping money is literally created out of thin air and is backed by central bank-issued paper redeemable in nothing.

There are two central truths about inflation: 1. Inflation is an increase in the money supply and 2. Credit is money. All other things being equal, an increase in the money supply will cause prices to rise while a contraction of the money supply will cause prices to fall.

In almost all countries today, central bank policy and the money supply are controlled by a small elite group. When this group increases the money supply, society as a whole does not benefit. The opposite is true. It is government and the establishment controlling it that benefit from access to newly created money. And when it is spent, the purchasing power of existing monetary units decreases. This new purchasing power is stolen goods. It does not create any new wealth nor any real honest demand. Real demand is created by producing what the free market will pay for. The ability to exchange real production is real demand. Inflating the money supply does not create any new service or product.

Spending by the holders of newly created money masquerades as real demand from the income of the politically well-connected when in fact it is capital stolen from the holders of existing monetary units. Taxing by theft of the purchasing power of existing money is the most devious and dishonest way to raise government revenue. It harms honest savers and elevates theft to statecraft. The government sets a very bad example. The harm done far exceeds any other form of taxation. It misallocates resources by sending false signals to economic players during the boom phase and thus results in serious misallocation of resources that must necessarily be liquidated during the bust phase.

It is true that you can keep warm by burning your neighbor's furniture in the fireplace, but you should not therefore conclude that you've discovered a new economic law that will result in permanently high share or real estate prices. It is very dangerous to base your financial planning on such illusions. If enough people are deluded by such fallacious reasoning, it may even result in a worldwide financial crisis.

The money fallacy persists for three major reasons. The first is historical. All money has its origins in the marketplace as the most accepted commodity for use in indirect exchange. Gold and silver have historically enjoyed the widest acceptance as commodity money. They are valued for use in ornamentation, dentistry, electronics, etc. They are useful as a medium of exchange, a unit of account, and a store of value.

With Nixon's closing of the gold window at the New York Federal Reserve on August 15, 1971, the US$ lost its last link to gold as did all currencies tied to the US$, meaning those of the forty-four Allied nations that signed the Bretton Woods Agreement in 1944. Curiously, the reserve status of the US$, though battered, has continued more or less intact until now. How can this be explained?

Governments are not able to define what money is, but once the marketplace defines money, governments are able to debase it. Today, through legal tender laws, they can force people to accept paper receipts as money in part because the receipts were once good for the delivery of a certain amount of gold or silver. This is true even though the receipts are no longer redeemable for anything.

The public does not yet fully understand that today's paper money does not have the commodity value of gold or silver, that in reality, it has no commodity value beyond the value of paper. The fact that the US$ was once a receipt for gold supports the fallacy that an increase in the amount of monetary units increases wealth. This was partly true when the monetary unit was gold. It is not true of today's money.

Failure to understand this truth contributes to support of policies calling for monetary inflation.

The second reason this money illusion exists is because people tend to and want to believe that what is good for them as individuals is good for everyone in society. It is true that if I receive a sum of newly created money and spend it to buy a house, car, etc., my living standard increases. It is not true, however, that this increases the living standard of society as a whole. The swimming pool analogy applies here. The increase in the money supply did nothing to increase the amount of goods and services produced, nor did it do anything to create new demand. It merely stole part of the purchasing power of existing monetary units and transferred it to the politically well-connected at the expense of everyone else. It isn't always true that what is to the advantage of one person is to the advantage of the group. Greed may distort perception, but a distorted perception does not change reality.

The third illusion is the fallacy of the Good Tsar, Our Dear Leader, and all other forms of idol worship including substituting the State for G-d. The illusion that the ruling group has society's interests at heart is essential to the continued rule of the establishment. If the common person knew that he was being milked by a parasitic ruling cabal, the establishment would soon be replaced. Slavery is dependent on the consent of the slave. This is true of all forms of exploitation and oppression. In a democracy, consent is engineered through control over mass media. It appears that consent has seriously deteriorated during the current financial crisis and multi-trillion dollar transfers to the establishment ruling class. Still, on balance, the illusion is holding. Obama has been served up as the new icon worthy of worldwide mass worship and it appears that a large proportion of the American and world public have accepted him as such.

To summarize, the money illusion is the fallacy that a society can increase its gross domestic product, its well-being, by increasing the money supply. This illusion has wide support within society because of the erroneous belief in the following.

1. The historical fallacy: What was true about money used in the past is true about money used today or, there is an inherent value in today's money beyond the value of paper.

2. The what is good for the individual is good for society as a whole fallacy or, one person's ability to steal the purchasing power of the larger group's money supply is good for society.

3. The idolatry fallacy. That our esteemed rulers have our best interests at heart or, that those who have organized and operate a deceptive banking system have done so and continue to do so for the benefit of society and not for their own narrow interests.

The truth is not complex. Real demand is created by production. Today's money can do no more than merely facilitate the exchange of one person's production for another person's production. It is not otherwise useful because it is not a commodity. Monetary inflation is used to steal the purchasing power of existing money. Government policy promotes and protects this theft for the benefit of the establishment that controls government. The money illusion is used to hide these truths.

Money is one half of every transaction. The monopoly right to issue a nation's currency is the most valued and has historically been the most fought over political privilege. Since the issuance of new monetary units steals the purchasing power of existing units it is necessary to hide what is really happening, namely theft. This is why 97 percent of what is written about economics is deliberately intended to mislead. If you understand what is really happening, you have a significant advantage in investing, business, and life. There are economic laws as immutable as the law of gravity and there are economic cycles related to sun spots, weather, and human emotions. Unless, however, you are reading the three percent of what is written that is true, you will be at a very serious disadvantage to those who know the facts and so understand what is really happening. In making investment decisions, we are competing with everyone else. Knowing what most people do not know is desirable. Knowing what decisions people are making based on illusion is important. They will most likely lose money. Being on the other side of their trade should be profitable.

A panic occurs when people realize that the wealth is gone. The wealth was stolen years earlier when the newly created money was spent. Today's panic is simply the emotional reaction to that realization. If you do not suffer from the money illusion, you will understand. There is no—zero—possibility of increasing living standards for society as a whole by repeating the earlier theft through more monetary inflation as most of the world's governments are now doing. When a critical mass of people understands this, paper money will be rejected and the crack-up boom will begin. At that point, paper money may quickly lose all value and the establishment may be forced to introduce a new currency backed by real value. Alternatively, we may see the introduction of a new totalitarianism and a long and deep depression. Current government responses do not bode well for an early end to the crisis. The one exception is Iran. In 2008, Iran spent US$75 billion to convert all its foreign currency reserves to gold and it is not keeping that gold in European or American banks. If it starts minting gold coins, we may see a new world reserve currency emerge. The empire will not permit this without a fight. In 2012, Brazil, Russia, India, China, and South Africa signed an agreement to trade using local currencies instead of US dollars. Several alternatives to the SWIFT interbank financial communication system are in place and ready to compete with or replace it; these pose a real threat to US dollar hegemony. Perhaps World War III has already started. China and Russia are on Iran's side. Israel is on the USA side.

CHAPTER V

The Sovereign Debt Crises
We Promise to Pay You Unless We Decide not to

Given a free market choice, very few people would buy so-called sovereign debt, i.e., government debt. That is one reason why central banks create money out of thin air and use it to buy the debt. But let us take a look at what's happening, ignoring the group fictions and analyzing it from the perspective of individual human action.

Politicians and bureaucrats borrow the money to pay themselves large salaries and to advance the interests of the financiers controlling the politicians. They want the system to continue for their benefit. Then there are buyers of the debt—bankers—who get large bonuses and enormous power from controlling the private issuance of government money.

They also want the system to continue for their benefit and are willing, or have been willing, to kill to protect the status quo. When there is a problem, the banks get bailed out. Who pays for this? The bankers and politicians want taxpayers to pay. In early 2012, taxpayers in Athens burned down 45 buildings. They were also willing to kill. Was that the beginning of a war to determine the sovereign: big banks and parliamentary deputies or taxpayers and the new revolutionaries? Discontent is rising throughout the EU. Populist and separatist movements are gaining ground in southern as well as northern member states; the United Kingdom could be the first to leave. The Union's eventual dissolution might be inevitable; the question is whether or not it will be peaceful.

Many doomsayers predict a new world order in which most of the population is reduced to servitude and poverty. We do not believe that's what the future holds. We are optimistic. The world is far more prosperous and free now than it was 50, 100, or 250 years ago. We are of the view that Karl Marx got one thing right: political systems are a reflection of the economic system. We are in the information age and the information age requires freedom. It is possible to destroy the Internet but not without paying an enormous economic price. With this in mind, let's explore how to profit from information and what we have learned so far.

To begin, let's take a look at a famous stock operator and his approach to uncovering opportunities for profit. Jesse Lauriston Livermore (1877 - 1940), known as the "Great Bear of Wall Street", made and lost several fortunes in the stock market. He used a system he began to develop at age fourteen when working an entry-level position at a brokerage in Boston. He analyzed price and volume data and became expert at predicting whether a stock or commodity would rise or fall. Livermore played both long and short positions because both offered opportunity for profit. He made his biggest fortunes during the crashes of 1907 and 1929. In each instance, he understood that the existing overextension of credit in the market would inevitably result in falling prices. He accordingly short sold and made 3 million and 100 million dollars in each crash respectively.

Livermore traded solely on his own account, devoting much effort and time to improving his skills. Evolving his strategy, learning from experience, and remaining flexible were keys to his success, and it is possible that failing to do so led to difficulties later in life. His approach was tactical and thorough. He conducted due diligence and kept track of price patterns and trade volume. He observed that the majority of traders allowed fear and hope to interfere with their trading decisions. Fear made them exit a winning position before making big profits, and hope made them hold onto a losing position when they should sell. Livermore employed the opposite strategy. He advised traders to fear a loss developing into a much bigger loss, and to hope a profit would grow into a much bigger profit.

Livermore's trading rules and lessons include the following:

- Ignore tips; rely instead on your own judgment, strategy, and analysis.
- Learn how to lose. Losing trades offer an invaluable education as long as you learn from them.
- Study underlying market conditions and trends. Trade with the trend; buy in a bull market and short in a bear market.
- Only trade when there are clear opportunities. If none exist, do not take any action.
- Never risk capital losses of more than 10 percent. If you lose your stake, you're out of the game.

- Wait for the market to confirm your opinion before entering a trade. Patience is the key to big profits.
- Continue with trades that show a profit and close trades that show a loss. Good trades usually show a profit from the beginning.
- Exit trades where the prospect for further profits is minimal.
- In any sector, trade the leading stock, the one showing the strongest trend. Trade the strongest stocks in a bull market or the weakest stocks in a bear market.
- Limit the number of stocks you follow. Don't scatter your attention; instead, focus on what matters.

These rules refer specifically to trading in the stock market, but Livermore's general recommendations can easily be applied to all kinds of earning opportunities. In the next chapter, we'll explore how government obstruction in the free market creates opportunity for speculative profits. Livermore is a clear example of this phenomenon. He was hugely successful in 1929 because he was aware that the government manipulated credit markets through control of the banking system and understood the necessary results of that manipulation.

CHAPTER VI

A Closer Look at the Opportunity for Speculative Profits

Opportunity for speculative profit (OSP) exists in any situation where the difference between the free market price (FMP) and the government obstructed price (GOP) exceeds the cost of arbitrage (COA).

There are a number of useful ways to express this.

If FMP exceeds GOP plus COA then OSP exists.

Or,
$$FMP > GOP + COA = OSP$$

The syllogism would be:

Premise 1: If FMP exceeds GOP plus COA then OSP exists.
Premise 2: FMP exceeds GOP plus COA.
Conclusion: OSP exists.

Another way to express this when FMP is larger than GOP plus COA is to compute the amount of speculative profit (SP):

$$FMP - (GOP + COA) = SP$$

Also,
If GOP exceeds FMP plus COA then OSP exists.

Or,
$$GOP > FMP + COA = OSP$$

The syllogism would be:

Premise 1: If GOP exceeds FMP plus COA then OSP exists.
Premise 2: GOP exceeds FMP plus COA.
Conclusion: OSP exists.

Another way to express this when GOP is larger than FMP plus COA is to compute the amount of speculative profit (SP):

$$GOP - (FMP + COA) = SP$$

The general plan in each of the above two examples would be to buy in the low-priced market and sell into the high-priced market: buy low and sell high or sell high and buy low. The sequential order and way in which the transactions can occur depend on many factors including legal restrictions and practical considerations. This can best be understood by going through examples. First, let's review some points you may now accept from reading the book this far.

Only individual human beings act. Groups: government, society, banks, political parties, companies do not act. Only the individuals that are part of these groups act. All act in accordance with their perceived self-interest.

All governments are on a continuum of terror. Governments, or to be more precise, bureaucrats, politicians, and their paymasters, use force and the threat of force to advance their own perceived self-interest.

War is the underlying organizing principle of government. During the 20th century, not counting actual wars, approximately 200 million people were murdered by their own governments. Governments killed about eight times as many people as did private individuals. Offensive war, the initiation of the use of coercive force, is used by governments against their own residents.

The right to collect taxes is a war trophy. So is the right to issue the nation's currency. It is the most important war trophy.

Properly accounted for, both the USA and the Russian Federation spend more than fifty percent of their budgets on war, security, and interest on debts to pay for war. Governments are parasitic organizations that do not create any wealth. They impose their will by restricting free trade or by subsidizing conduct they wish to promote. This they do for the benefit of their paymasters, the establishment that controls government. Deception is essential to the continuation of this system. Propaganda and double agents are central to maintaining the deception.

All governmental action distorts the free market. Generally, when trade is restricted, prices increase and supply decreases. When something is subsidized, prices tend to decrease and supply increase.

Extraordinary speculative profits, profits in excess of the business and credit risks and time value of money, are available when there is a large discrepancy between the free market price and the price due to government interference and, the cost of arbitrage is low relative to the gain.

Taxation is a common way governments obstruct free markets. Most governments tax the income of their citizens and residents. If you own a 100-unit rental apartment house and collect rent from your 100 tenants you will generally have to include that in your taxable income and pay a tax on it. If, however, there are 100 people who own and live in the 100 apartments, no income tax is collected on the value of the rental in most jurisdictions. The 100 owners are getting the economic benefit of the rental value they are accruing to themselves by virtue of living in the apartment they own. There is a different tax treatment for the same asset, the 100 apartments, based only on who owns it and how it is used.

Let us assume now that all investors and homeowners investing in their own living quarters were willing to buy if they received a 10 percent yield on their investment. Also, let us assume that there is a 50 percent income tax that the owners of rental property would have to pay and that homeowners would not pay any tax on the economic value of the rents. Further, let us assume that the rental value of one apartment is 2,000 euros per year and that the cost to convert the rental apartments to owner-occupied apartments is 1,000 euros per apartment.

In the above example, is there opportunity for speculative profits (OSP)?

What is the free market price (FMP) of one apartment?

What is the government obstructed price (GOP) of one apartment?

What is the cost of arbitrage (COA) for one apartment?

The FMP of one apartment, assuming a 10 percent capitalization rate, would be 20,000 euros. Ten percent of 20,000 equals the rental value, 2,000 euros, to a homeowner who does not have to pay a tax on the rental value of the apartment.

The GOP of one apartment, assuming a 10 percent capitalization rate, would be 10,000 euros. The 2,000 euros rent would be subject to a 50 percent tax of 1,000 euros and so the net income would only be 1,000 euros. Ten percent of 10,000 euros is 1,000 euros.

So FMP, or 20K, less GOP, or 10K, equals 10K, or the profit before subtracting the cost of arbitrage. The cost of converting the rental apartments to owner-occupied apartments is the cost of the arbitrage or 1,000 euros per apartment. The full formula would be as follows.

20,000 euros (FMP) less 10,000 euros (GOP) less 1,000 euros (COA) equals 9,000 euros (OSP).

The opportunity for speculative profits from the 100-unit rental apartment house, based only on removing the government interference in the free market would be 900,000 euros. In order to earn this 900,000 euros, you would have to buy at the investment rental value and sell at the homeowner value with expenses of 100,000 euros to buy and resell.

The most common form of arbitrage to remove the effect of taxation is to deal in the cash market, black market, or free market. This includes smuggling and other dealings with contraband. Here, the cost of arbitrage may be very great as it can include the risk of government fines and imprisonment. There is also the corrosive moral degradation cost to one's inner self and ability to think clearly. All value is subjective. If your inner subjective self is ill, you will find it very difficult to value the components of economic calculations properly. These factors are difficult to quantify and so we will not, for the most part, discuss how to profit from petty crime. It is imperative, however, that you understand the economics of major criminal activities.

During the USA presidential election of 1912, the major banking interests financed both the Bull Moose Party, headed by Teddy Roosevelt seeking a third term, and the Democratic Party. They financed the Bull Moose Party to split the Republican Party vote and so assure Woodrow Wilson's election. Wilson had no significant prior political experience. He had been president of Princeton University. In return for the bankers' support, Wilson agreed to sign an act establishing the third USA private central bank, the Federal Reserve System.

For purposes of analyzing this situation, we will assume that in today's money it cost the bankers $500,000,000 to finance the Bull Moose Party and $1,000,000,000 to finance the Democratic Party. We will further assume that the bankers, up to the time of the 1912 election, had already spent $500,000,000 in pursuit of establishing their private central bank, and that the value of their existing banks was $100,000,000,000. From the foregoing we may wonder why the banking interests were willing to spend $2,000,000,000. Here we can apply the three laws of economics discussed earlier: 1. All value is subjective. 2. People prioritize their values. 3. The only way to judge a person's value scale is by observing what they do: buying and selling or not buying or selling.

Here the bankers paid $2b so we know that they valued what they got in return more than $2b. How much more? They got the monopoly right to issue the currency of the USA. They got the ability to create money out of thin air. They got the ability to prevent bank runs by issuing an unlimited amount of credit to themselves and anyone else they cared to. They became the real owners of America. For purposes of this example let us assume that's worth $10 trillion.

In the above example, is there opportunity for speculative profits (OSP)?

What is the free market price (FMP) of their banks?

What is the government obstructed price (GOP) of their banks?

What is the cost of arbitrage (COA)?

In this example the bankers did not buy or sell their banks. They increased the value of their banks by obtaining the monopoly powers that went with owning and controlling a private central bank.

Their OSP was the difference between the value of their banks with a monopoly power and the value without a monopoly power less the cost of getting the monopoly power.

GOP ($10t) less FMP ($100b) less COA ($2B) = SP ($9,898,000,000,000)

In this case they did not have to spend to buy the banks at their free market value. These they had from earlier investment. Incrementally they spent $2b to have a profit of whatever the value of a monopoly power added to their existing situation. With the above assumptions the rate of return was 4,949 percent. This is extraordinary speculative profit when measured against the monetary cost of transforming a free market banking system into a monopoly banking system. The benefit, however, accrued only to the owners and supporters of the new monopoly privileges. Everyone else paid and continues to pay. In a normal commercial transaction the speculator would buy in the low-priced market from the owner and sell into the high-priced market. Here they did not sell. Their earnings would continue for the duration of their monopoly. Also, they did not buy the monopoly privilege from the owners: the USA public. Instead they used the political process to steal it. It was a theft because the bankers did not pay the owners. Only one president has gone around the Federal Reserve System by issuing greenbacks directly from the treasury and he died 90 days later in Dallas, Texas. It is important to keep in mind who the real owners are. The USA dollar is approximately 65 percent of the world's central bank reserves. The monopoly distortion of the free market caused by the USA private central banking system's obstructive power is the largest single factor to consider when looking for speculative profits outside tax policy and war. France and England had private central banks until shortly after WWII. It appears that the same groups continue to control most of the large western banks and government policy today. The consequences of this restraint on trade are evident throughout the West's economies and present many opportunities for speculative profits.

Earlier, we characterized dealing in contraband as petty crime, but governments apply this term to innumerable circumstances, products, and services when they intervene in the free market. Often, a more accurate description of "dealing in contraband" might be "to circumvent government obstruction of an entire market or market segments." Some examples, both current and historical, are currencies, alcohol, cigarettes, gambling, pharmaceuticals, coffee, and sugar.

Let's say the year is 1979. In the USSR, the government obstructed price of one ruble is $1.65. Soviet law forbids entry into the country with rubles, meaning tourists are forced to buy the currency at this high price. You decide, however, the risk taken in defying Soviet law is worth the potential gain, buy rubles in Vienna, Austria, at the free market price of $0.31 per ruble and enter the USSR with the currency. In Leningrad, you use these rubles to buy caviar to take out of the country upon departure.

In this example, GOP is $1.65 and FMP is $0.31 while COA depends on your point of view. Arguably, there are real and psychological consequences to committing what Soviet law determines a crime. If discovered, the currency bought in Vienna could be confiscated as could the caviar bought with it. Soviet police could make real trouble for you. On the other hand, perhaps these considerations are negligible considering the gratification of defying an oppressive regime and the likelihood of success in completing your transactions and leaving the country with the purchased goods.

For our purposes, let's say COA is negligible. In this case, OSP exists.

GOP > FMP + COA = OSP

OSP per USSR ruble is the following:

GOP ($1.65) − [(FMP ($0.31) + COA (0)] = OSP ($1.34)

The difference between GOP and FMP is OSP ($1.34). Divide this by the FMP ($0.31) and you find the resulting profit is 432 percent. With FMP rubles, you are able to buy 4.32 times more caviar than with GOP rubles. You are able to sell FMP rubles into the GOP market for more than a respectable profit.

The following is another example of buying in a free market and selling in a government obstructed market. In this case, we can also characterize it as buying in a market that is more free and selling in a market that is less free while creating a freer market option in that second market. In the United Kingdom, the sale of children's clothing is exempt from VAT (Value Added Tax) while in Poland the VAT for this item is 23 percent. Poland's business regulatory environment also results in relatively high operating costs compared to the UK. These two factors contribute to higher retail prices in Poland. It is possible to buy designer brand children's clothing from a wholesale supplier in the UK at a much reduced cost to what retail customers pay for the same clothing in Poland.

You travel to the UK and buy children's cotton shirts in bulk at 3 euros per shirt which in Poland you sell for 10 euros each. Through word of mouth, your client list steadily grows because in Poland, the same quality shirt retails at 15 euros.

To calculate OSP, the formula is different here than in our previous examples because we are dealing with two free market prices: the one in the UK and the one you sell at when you create a freer market price option in Poland. If the first FMP plus the cost of arbitrage is less than the second FMP, then OSP exists.

$$FMP1 + COA < FMP2 = OSP$$

COA includes travel expenses between the two countries and the risk taken when VAT and other taxes are not paid in Poland. If we assume COA is 2 euros per shirt, the calculation would be

FMP1 (3 euros) + COA (2 euros) < FMP2 (10 euros) = OSP (5 euros).

This results in a profit of 100 percent.

A currency reset is another situation which can lead to OSP. Typically, governments take this action when prices, due to inflation of the money supply, have risen markedly over a period of time. The mechanism is simple. For example, in a 10:1 reset, holders of ten old paper currency units must exchange these for one new paper currency unit. The government decrees that all debts denominated in the old currency are now payable in 1/10 of the new currency units. The old paper currency's purchasing power remains the same, at least theoretically, but what happens to the old-issue coins? Often, coins are ignored in the reset process because few remain in active circulation. If this is the case, in this example, their purchasing power increases nine times.

With foresight, you can plan for an eventual reset by stocking up on coins. When the reset occurs, each old GOP coin with a one-unit denomination is now worth ten times one new GOP paper bill. COA is zero because you simply buy coins with equivalent GOP paper money before the reset. In this case,

$$GOP1 + COA < GOP2 = OSP$$

Or,

$$GOP2\ (10) - [GOP1\ (1) + COA\ (0)] = OSP\ (9)$$

This is a 900 percent profit, meaning the buying power of one old coin with the same face value as one new paper bill is ten times that of the new paper money.

If we take a closer look at Chapter III, we also see how foreign trusts can be used to take advantage of OSP. In large part, Hughes, Katz, and the Durands form their trusts in order to safeguard income and property from taxation. In Hughes' case, one goal is to protect the value of his rental properties from future UK inheritance taxes. The FMP of his rental properties is their fair market value while the GOP is fair market value minus the 40 percent inheritance tax his heirs would have to pay if the properties weren't protected by trust ownership. COA is the minimal cost of setting up and maintaining the trust and offshore company.

Here, we have $FMP > GOP + COA = OSP$.

Katz uses her trust to form an offshore company that conducts business with her Haifa company. The trust-held offshore company is profitable while the Haifa company has low or negligible profits. In this way, Katz pays little income tax in her home country. The FMP of her income (or FMI: free market income) is higher than the GOP of her income (or GOI: government obstructed income). Again, COA is the nominal cost of setting up and operating the trust and offshore company. Here,

$$FMP \ (FMI) > GOP \ (GOI) + COA = OSP$$

The Durands also capitalize on the difference between FMI and GOI when they periodically wire undeclared income to their Caribbean trust account. With wise investment, the Durands see their savings grow.

Insider Short Selling

It is against the law in most countries for a person deemed an insider to short sell his company's shares. Public company officers and directors are insiders and have a fiduciary obligation to look after the financial interests of the company and its shareholder owners. To make money on selling the shares short violates this duty in appearance and fact. In addition to criminal penalties, it is generally the rule that any profits an insider makes from such short selling activity must be paid over to the company for the benefit of all shareholders. Some owners do not believe they should be constrained by the law as it applies to the public. Being the real owners, they feel entitled to profit from knowing their company will issue a bad report in the near future. One method of circumventing these short selling rules is as follows.

An issuing bank in another jurisdiction sells its midterm notes with the interest rate and/or principal repayment tied to the price of the first bank's share price. If the shares of the first bank are now 50, and the price at the end of the term of the notes is 65, the holder of the note

89

gets a premium of 30 percent. If the share price is higher than 65, the premium is still limited to 30 percent. If, however, the price of the shares dips to 5, the holder of the note only gets back 10 percent and the issuer bank keeps the difference: 90 percent. Economically this is a short sale with limitation of possible loss to the short seller of 30 percent.

The owners apparently feel that since profit is taken out through a midterm note and not through a direct short sale of the first bank's shares, and the mechanism for the short sale is in a second jurisdiction in the form of a debt instrument, the law against profiting from short selling your company's shares does not apply. Perhaps they feel above the law since they own both countries through controlling the major banks in both jurisdictions, meaning they control the regulators, police, politicians, prosecutors, judges, and jailers in both jurisdictions. If you are offered a very large block of the midterm notes nine months before the due date and the shares of the first bank are trading at 50, what should you do? What should you do if the number of notes in the block offered to you exceeds the number of issued and outstanding notes?

In the foregoing example, the most likely situation is that the insiders have shorted and want to short more shares of the first bank. In view of the complexity woven and the amount of securities for sale, it is very likely the securities are being offered by insiders. If the insiders wish to be massively short the shares, what is the likely direction of the share price? If the insiders have erected an elaborate structure that is at best borderline legal in order to short the shares of their company, what is the likely direction of the share price over the next nine months?

All of the names and some of the facts have been withheld or changed to protect the less than innocent. The game appears to have been fixed. Insiders are short the shares and want to short more. The incremental cost of being short is the expense of issuing the midterm notes. Maintaining their ownership of two countries permits multiple opportunities for profit through corruption and theft. Were they to lose that control, they might be subject to criminal prosecution for their scheme.

What will be the market price of the first bank's shares nine months out? If we are correct in our analysis that the game is fixed, we can surmise it will be less than today's price and the cost of maintaining the short position.

Can the above example be fitted into any of the formulae we have discussed so far?

What is the FMP?

What is the GOP?

What is the COA?

Is there OSP?

It appears that OSP exists for the issuers and short sellers of the midterm notes if the share price of the first bank decreases over the next nine months. The COA would be the cost of doing the short sale. For the owners, that would be the incremental cost of issuing the midterm notes. It would not be practical to engage in this sort of scheme unless you were an owner of both countries. It may be that the FMP of the first bank's shares is zero. If that is the case, any price above zero would be the GOP. If you disregard the earnings major establishment banks accrued which were possible only because of their monopoly privilege, over the last 50 years, they have all lost money. They are capital destruction entities. The 2008 bailouts clearly showed that many of them were bankrupt. This was also the case in 1980 if you marked to market all assets on the balance sheets of the major money center banks in the USA.

This doesn't mean the banks were worthless to everyone. The insiders have benefited enormously. In the last case, we can see they've been able to circumvent the prohibition against insiders shorting their own company's shares. It is not that they are above the law. They are the law, at least until a revolution changes this fact. They are following their own perceived self-interest. They are using the art of war to obstruct the laws of economics. They will continue to do this as long as they perceive it to be in their self-interest. The cost of maintaining the existing system is low relative to the insiders' gain. When this changes, so will the system.

In the last instance: GOP is 50, FMP is 0 and COA is say 2. The formula presentation on a per share basis for the insiders would be:

$$GOP\ (50) - [(FMP\ (O) + COA\ (2)] = OSP\ (48)$$

It is unlikely the insiders would permit the share price to fall to zero as this might mean losing control over a key element of their governance.

What should the person wishing to take advantage of this information do?

From the above, it appears highly probable that the price of the first bank will significantly decrease over the next nine months. Short sale of the shares is one option, shorting the call option is another, buying the put option is a third, and shorting the midterm notes is a fourth possibility.

Based on the above it may be there's an 80 percent or better chance the shares will substantially decline in the next nine months. Find another nine such stocks and you have a very interesting situation. Perhaps you can find nine more midterm notes that are tied to a share price. Perhaps you can review the past performance of midterm notes tied to a share price to give you an indication of what's really happening.

CHAPTER VII

Putting It All Together

You now have a foundation in economic law and the art of war. You have seen how these principles can be applied for financial gain, and are familiar with real world examples of their application. But knowledge alone is not enough. Unless that knowledge is put to use, it will do little good. In fact, it is only through taking action that anything can be fully known. Action builds, expands, and anchors what is known at the mental level—knowledge together with action results in deeper knowledge and success. But it is necessary to take the correct action. Therefore, one might ask: Is it possible to evaluate whether an action taken or considered is the correct action to take? Can the likelihood of taking the right action be increased?

Fortunately, the answer is yes. Choosing a direction and destination for one's financial, business, and personal life is vital. When action is taken consciously, it is the act of implementing a goal in order to go in a determined direction and reach a determined destination. In reality, only two options are possible: to make a decision and take a particular action or to make no decision and allow circumstances to dictate what action is taken. Clearly, a method for evaluating whether the destination chosen is attainable would be useful. And if this method can be applied to one's own goals as well as those of other people upon whom one depends, this would be very useful indeed.

Sun Tzu demonstrates that the best way to win a war is to do so before the first battle begins. The same can be said of one's ultimate success. It is necessary to determine which goals and interactions with others are productive and which are not. It is best to use energy resources wisely; more time should be spent on goals and interactions that are likely to increase financial and personal well-being. The following systems will help you do just that. You are ready to take action. It is time to ensure your chances of success just as Sun Tzu and Jesse Livermore ensured theirs.

Five Steps for Predicting Human Behavior

Often, people say they will take a particular course of action, make a commitment to do so, but then fail to follow through. Or, they make every effort to reach the determined objective but have no success. Why are they unable to achieve an end they know, objectively, would benefit them? The answer is simple: Objectively knowing is not enough. There are three other factors involved, and all three must be fulfilled in order to attain a goal. First, a person needs to think he can achieve it. Second, he must feel he can—want to—achieve it. And third, reality has to support his goal. The five-step system for predicting human behavior approaches goal setting from this perspective. It recognizes that mind, emotions, and reality all play a part in reaching goals. Use it to set goals you're more likely to attain. Use it to understand other people's behavior and whether or not they are likely to do what they say they will do.

Start by defining your goal. What precisely do you want to achieve? Be specific. The more time you spend on this the better. It is also highly beneficial to picture yourself having already attained your goal; hold an image in your mind that is specific and detailed. Consider the questions what, when, who, and where. Once this is done, ask yourself the following.

1. Do you think you can achieve it?
2. Do you feel you can achieve it?
3. Is truth on your side?
4. Is there sufficient emotion?
5. Is there sufficient truth?

Ask yourself what else might be needed to reach the goal.

If the answer is no at any step, the goal will not be reached. A positive final outcome requires a yes at all steps. And this yes needs to be correct; meaning the process of evaluation must lead to an accurate answer. If chances are only 50/50 that the yes answer is correct for each question, a favorable result is only a 3.125% probability. This explains why people often say they will do something and then do not do it.

This system recognizes that mind, emotions, and reality, and how you act and react in relation to these factors, determine success or failure in business and life in general.

This should be fairly obvious. If a person doesn't think he can win a race, it is unlikely he will enter it; or if he enters the race, he will work subconsciously to fulfill a mental picture of not winning.

If a person doesn't feel she can win a race, the energy isn't there to make it happen. First comes the mental decision, the thinking you can do it, that opens or closes the door, and then comes the emotion—Step 2—that provides the force to drive through the door. Understanding this will help you remember to be consistently positive when you want to accomplish a task or goal.

But the open door and your ability to drive through it are not enough. You also need to be realistic. If there is a cliff on the other side of the door and you continue to move forward, you are going to fall off that cliff. This will happen even though you thought you could—Step 1—and felt you could—Step 2—because the laws of gravity are part of the truth—Step 3—that must be on your side.

Step 4 is sufficient emotions, sufficient to the task and its completion. This is not a simple repetition of Step 2 when you reflected on your inner emotional state. This step requires you to analyze all external factors to ensure there's enough fuel in the tank to get where you want to go.

Similarly, Step 5 is not a repetition of Step 3. You now need to be sure that sufficient truth is on your side to complete the task. Perhaps you need a plane instead of a car. Maybe you need to use calculus rather than arithmetic.

This system sheds light on your current mental, emotional, and factual situation and on what you need to succeed, or if success is possible at all. You might need to revise your short-term goals in order to reach the final goal using the quickest route.

It also reveals why people say they will do something and then don't do it. A person may think she will but not realize she doesn't have sufficient emotions—Step 4—to do the required task. Or, she may not understand she needs a plane rather than a car to reach her goal or get there on time—Step 5. Or, a person may be so disconnected from his feelings he will tell you he'll do something because he thinks—Step 1— he will even though he does not really feel—Step 2—that he can. If he tells you he will when he thinks he cannot—Step 1—he is simply lying. Ask a few pertinent questions, keeping in mind the five steps, and it is often possible to accurately predict failure or success.

Five Steps for Managing Human Relations

Reaching a goal often requires cooperation from other people. Therefore, how you manage your relations with others will determine, in large part, how successful you are at accomplishing goals. All personal and business interactions benefit from understanding human behavior and motivations. Realizing this will help you focus your efforts on profitable action and use your time wisely. Whether your goal is to sell apartments, decide how to share family household chores, or increase employee productivity, similar conditions must exist for potential buyers to become actual buyers, for an agreement that everyone will honor to be reached, and for your employees to be more effective. If these conditions do not exist, there is little likelihood of reaching your goal in that particular situation.

Success is more than simply reaching an objective; its definition is broader. Success does not require attaining a particular objective every time or with every person. Success may more accurately be defined as reaching the best possible outcome in the shortest amount of time while expending the least amount of energy. Energy resources include time. Effective management of human relations ensures effective management of your own time and greatly increases the likelihood of success.

Following this five-step system allows you to focus on opportunities most likely to result in a positive outcome.

1. Attention. It should be obvious that getting an individual's attention is the first step. Nothing can be done without it. In a one-on-one sales situation, repeat the prospective client's name and offer a handshake. On the phone, smile like you would in the individual's presence. Your attention is just as important as theirs. It shows you value the person you're speaking with and give importance to the situation; it invites that person to do the same. Arrange a time that everyone agrees on to talk about household chores. Arrange a meeting with each supervisor to discuss productivity. If you do not have the individual's attention, do not go forward.

2. Qualification. This step does not always apply. Your teenage children live with you and are most likely capable of cleaning dishes and walking the dog. But ask the prospective client questions to confirm he's able to buy from you. Make sure he has the financial means. Find out whether anyone else such as a spouse is involved in buying the apartment. If he isn't qualified, there is no sense in taking the next step. Your time and energy are valuable.

3. Interests. Ask questions. Find out what interests the prospective client, family member(s), or supervisor(s) and employee(s). Listen. Pay attention. This isn't the time to sell your product or idea. That happens in Step 4. You need to know what motivates the individual before you can know how to convince him or her to buy what you're selling. So again, listen carefully. Pay attention.

4. Desire. This is when you try to convince the individual that what you are selling advances his or her interests. Use the information

gained in Step 3 to build up the individual's desire in Step 4. Emotion is required for thought (interests) to turn into action. Show how your product, service, or idea will help the individual get what he or she already wants. This is the only way someone will agree to do something he or she wouldn't normally do without your intervention. This is the heart of effective sales and management. Without sufficient desire, there is no point in going further. Use your time and energy wisely. If this means focusing your attention on another client, then that's what you should do.

5. Close: Get the contract signed and money transferred to the seller's account or the chore schedule written and accepted. To reach a goal that requires cooperation from many people, like increased employee productivity, you need to follow a less direct path. Get the supervisors to commit to doing business differently while they in turn get employees to commit to the same. The five steps will be used several times in this process. For instance, what supervisors learn about employees' interests in Step 3 will help you refine your strategy.

If the answer is no to the close, this usually means something was missed in Steps 1 through 4. You will need to go back to properly handle the issue(s) before returning to Step 5.

Follow this procedure exactly and in the provided order; otherwise you risk wasting your own time and that of the prospective client, family member, or employee.

Remember that success means reaching the best possible outcome in the shortest time while expending the least amount of energy. Everyone wants to be effective in his or her personal and business life. Using these five steps to manage human relations will ensure you focus your efforts efficiently and get the best possible results.

CONCLUSION

Extraordinary speculative profits are possible with minor risk if you verify the truth, properly use logic, and keep it private. The establishment will continue to make war and milk the public. If you understand exactly how they are doing this, you can protect yourself and profit far beyond the norm. If you are short selling shares that the establishment is short, your risk level is low and potential for profit high. This is not investment activity or undertaking a market risk. It is speculative profit in time of civil war.

Properly done, short sellers have less risk and more potential gain than insiders. The key is to have good information. Because the speculator does not bear the insider's cost of promotion, his risk is less and his potential for gain greater than even the establishment insider.

The successful speculator applies critical thinking to the truth. Armed with an understanding of economic law and the factors affecting economic freedom, as well as the skills necessary to analyze and choose your actions wisely, you are now ready to do just that. It won't always be easy, but it will always be worthwhile.

APPENDIX

Formulae

For reference purposes, the following are economic formulae used in this book and a definition of the abbreviations contained in them.

OSP: opportunity for speculative profits

FMP: free market price

COA: cost of arbitrage

SP: speculative profit

GOP: government obstructed price

FMI: free market income

GOI: government obstructed income

      1. If FMP exceeds GOP plus COA, OSP exists.
Or,
FMP > GOP + COA = OSP
FMP − (GOP + COA) = SP

      2. If GOP exceeds FMP plus COA, OSP exists.
Or,
GOP > FMP + COA = OSP
GOP − (FMP + COA) = SP

3. If the first FMP plus COA is less than the second FMP, OSP exists.

Or,

FMP1 + COA < FMP2 = OSP

4. If the first GOP plus COA is less than the second GOP, OSP exists.

Or,

GOP1 + COA < GOP2 = OSP

5. If FMI exceeds GOI plus COA, OSP exists.

Or,

FMI > GOI + COA = OSP

www.ingramcontent.com/pod-product-compliance
Lightning Source LLC
Chambersburg PA
CBHW060358190526
45169CB00002B/656